"Based on the finest scientific evide: guide for teens with post-traumatic stress disorder (PTSD) is an outstanding resource for those who are exposed to violence and traumatic events. It's an exceptional book for its clarity and for its readability. Therapists, parents, and teens themselves will benefit from including this guide in their efforts to overcome trauma and PTSD. This belongs in every therapist's resource library. It is a rich toolbox for successful care for teens with PTSD."

> —**Terence M. Keane, PhD**, director of the behavioral science division of the National Center for PTSD, and professor and assistant dean of research at the Boston University School of Medicine

"This book by a psychologist/mother and daughter team speaks clearly and wisely to teens (and their parents) about the expectable but often otherwise misunderstood aftermath of experiencing traumatic stressors. By blending state-of-the-art research and therapeutic insights with the voices of teens, this book provides a refreshing and very useful guide to resilience in the wake of trauma."

> —**Julian D. Ford, PhD, ABPP**, professor of psychiatry and law, director of the Center for Trauma Recovery and Juvenile Justice, director of the Center for the Treatment of Developmental Trauma Disorders, and associate editor of the *Journal of Trauma & Dissociation* and the *European Journal of Psychotraumatology*

"Sheela Raja and Jaya Ashrafi have crafted an exceptionally well done and timely book that will no doubt be an invaluable resource and comfort to teen survivors of trauma. For far too long, the trauma self-help literature has been geared toward an exclusively adult audience and we have neglected the needs of teenagers who are similarly afflicted, and we have failed to support their efforts to engage in adaptive self-care. The authors distill state-of-the-science treatment principles in an approachable, nontechnical format that teens will find accessible and engaging. Sheela Raja's extensive research and clinical expertise with traumatic stress ensures that the advice offered is sound, and supported by the best available research. Jaya Ashrafi—a teen author—offers a perspective that is especially insightful, and ensures that the content is approachable and relevant for teen readers. Their combined efforts have yielded a critically important resource for teens impacted by trauma. I highly recommend it."

—**Matt J. Gray, PhD**, professor of clinical psychology at the University of Wyoming; vice-chair of the Wyoming State Board of Psychology and the Wyoming Coalition Against Domestic Violence and Sexual Assault

"This is a necessary and ever so timely body of work. Now more than ever, our teens are exposed to trauma, whether in their personal lives, their communities, or through world events. Understanding PTSD in this context empowers teenagers, their parents, and professionals. The mother-daughter duo of Sheela Raja and Jaya Ashrafi together create a workbook that is informative, accessible, and practical. Jaya's succinct perspectives provide a unique window into the mind of today's teens. In total, this book engages the reader while promoting self-reflection, skill building, and resilience. A must-read for any adolescent who has experienced trauma."

> **—Shairi R. Turner, MD, MPH**, chief medical officer at Crisis Text Line

the ***instant*** *help*
solutions series

Young people today need mental health resources more than ever. That's why New Harbinger created the **Instant Help Solutions Series** especially for teens. Written by leading psychologists, physicians, and professionals, these evidence-based self-help books offer practical tips and strategies for dealing with a variety of mental health issues and life challenges teens face, such as depression, anxiety, bullying, eating disorders, trauma, and self-esteem problems.

Studies have shown that young people who learn healthy coping skills early on are better able to navigate problems later in life. Engaging and easy-to-use, these books provide teens with the tools they need to thrive—at home, at school, and on into adulthood.

This series is part of the **New Harbinger Instant Help Books** imprint, founded by renowned child psychologist Lawrence Shapiro. For a complete list of books in this series, visit newharbinger.com.

the **ptsd survival guide** for **teens**

strategies to **overcome trauma, build resilience & take back your life**

SHEELA RAJA, PhD
JAYA RAJA ASHRAFI

Instant Help Books
An Imprint of New Harbinger Publications, Inc.

Publisher's Note

INSTANT HELP, the Clock Logo, and NEW HARBINGER are trademarks of New Harbinger Publications, Inc.

New Harbinger Publications is an employee-owned company

Distributed in Canada by Raincoast Books

Copyright © 2018 by Sheela Raja and Jaya Ashrafi
                         Instant Help Books
                         An imprint of New Harbinger Publications, Inc.
                         5674 Shattuck Avenue
                         Oakland, CA 94609
                         www.newharbinger.com

Cover design by Amy Shoup

Acquired by Tesilya Hanauer

Edited by Cindy Nixon

Library of Congress Cataloging-in-Publication Data on file

Printed in the United States of America

25   24   23

10   9   8   7   6   5   4   3

For Leila and Nur

Contents

Contents

Introduction

If you are picking up this book, you have probably been through something difficult or very traumatic in your life. This introductory section will help you understand the various kinds of stress people experience and figure out which parts of this book will help you the most. Although our lives are full of day-to-day stressors, like dealing with a bad grade or having a fight with a friend, some stressors are far more serious. Stressors that are unexpected, life-threatening, and very intense are called *traumatic*. Traumatic stressors, also called *traumatic events*, can include things like living through a serious accident or natural disaster, witnessing violence at home or in your community, experiencing the sudden death or serious illness of a loved one, or being physically or sexually hurt in some way. Sadly, many of these events are very common in our culture. The good news is that we have more awareness about the seriousness of traumatic events than ever before, and we also have a lot more tools to help people recover. If you have experienced a traumatic event, please know that you are not alone. There is love and support out there for you, and you have the strength to live a meaningful, fulfilling life. This book can help you find that support and provide you with some tools for healing.

It is a brave decision to face what is bothering you, and you should know that you do not have to heal all by yourself. You can read this book on your own or use it with a therapist or other trusted adult. Sometimes, we think that we can just "get over" these kinds of events by not thinking about them. Perhaps others have told you—or you have told yourself—that you need to move on. But how? Starting to heal from something that is bothering you can be extremely difficult, but it is also extremely courageous. By taking a look at your thoughts, feelings, and behaviors, you can develop your strengths, build connections to supportive people, and find healthy ways to deal with challenges. But first, take a minute to congratulate yourself for being brave enough to think about your challenges—that isn't easy!

This book will give you information, but it will also give you a teen's perspective on how to apply that information to your life. Because teens face unique challenges and have some really great advantages (for example, you are usually less set in your ways than older people), we decided to write this book as a mother-daughter team. Sheela is a clinical psychologist with decades of experience in working with survivors of violence and trauma. Jaya is a teenager with a love of writing, a passion for helping people, and a strong belief that every kid and teenager deserves love and respect. Together, we hope to provide you with lots of information, show you how other teens have survived and thrived after trauma, and give you some specific techniques to try on your own journey of healing. While Sheela provides the technical information and gives you case examples (that have been changed somewhat to protect privacy) on how teens can heal, Jaya gives you a teen's perspective on the issues. Know that there is more than one path to healing. You can try things out and personalize what works for you, because no two journeys are the same. But still, you do not have to walk this road all by yourself. Before tackling specific issues, here's some basic information about stress and trauma, so you can better understand what you are dealing with.

What Is Stress?

We often hear the word "stress," but it is hard to figure out what it means. Is it good or bad? Does stress hurt our bodies? Can we recover from it? The answers to these questions depend on the kind of stress we are experiencing.

Manageable Stress

Life is full of stress, and most of it is *manageable stress*— the day-to-day hassles of life, school, friends, and activities. Manageable stress affects your mind and body for a brief period of time. For example, when you worry about doing well on an exam or winning a basketball game, your body gets "pumped up" and ready to deal with the challenge ahead. When you are faced with these short periods of stress, your body responds using the *fight-or-flight* mechanism that involves parts of your nervous system. You may find that your heart rate is fast and that you are sweating more. Overall, the body goes back to normal fairly quickly once you've dealt with manageable stress.

We often think of stress as a bad thing, but the body's short-term response to stress actually helps us to live and to stay safe. For example, if we are crossing the street and a car comes close to hitting us, we experience stress for several minutes. That is a good thing. It is our body's way of giving us the energy to get away from a dangerous situation and our mind's way of figuring out how to keep us out of danger in the future.

Tolerable Stress

When stress is more severe or ongoing, things get more complicated. *Tolerable stress* is longer lasting, and it's usually in response to something more serious. For example, you might have experienced the death of loved one, a natural disaster, or dealing with a serious illness in your family or yourself. The key here is social support. If you have people around you whom you can talk to and count on, these kinds of stressors are difficult, but they might not feel overwhelming after a few months have passed.

Toxic or Traumatic Stress

Finally, there are stressors that are considered *toxic* or *traumatic*, especially for kids and teens. This kind of stress is the result of situations that either are really intense or go on for a long period of time, and they can be very challenging for a young person—for instance, physical or sexual abuse, neglect, living in poverty, dealing with violence in your school or home, or having a parent or caregiver who is abusing substances or dealing with a mental illness. These events can be particularly difficult if you don't have a supportive and trusted adult in your life. Toxic or traumatic stressors can actually change the way your body functions and, over time, leave you feeling emotionally and physically exhausted.

It's important for you to know that you didn't deserve for these things to happen to you. They're not your fault. The good news is that people can survive and even thrive after living through situations like these. A key part of healing from them is identifying your strengths, learning healthy coping strategies, and developing a really strong support system. This book will help you try to do all of these things.

> ✳ **Jaya Says** ✳ *I think that manageable stress is pretty common for people my age, and I know I often deal with it. People I know have opened up to me about the different, more serious types of stress that they've experienced. Sometimes, I can see that they're acting differently or being more closed off when they are stressed about something, or they're thinking about something else when I'm trying to have a conversation with them.*

What Is Post-Traumatic Stress?

Post-traumatic stress is a set of reactions to toxic or traumatic events. In teens, these events can include:

* Sexual or physical abuse

* Other violent crimes

* School shootings

* Bullying

* Natural disasters

* Car crashes

* A loved one's suicide

* Living with violence in your home

* Living with violence in your community

Although you may feel like you are the only one, many teens, unfortunately, have experienced these types of events. Based on the results of various surveys and the types of trauma specified on them, as few as one in ten and as many as one in three young people have experienced a traumatic event. You are not alone.

There is also a common myth that experiencing lots of trauma means that difficult things won't bother you as much. If you've been through several traumatic events, it is true that you might feel increasingly numb or cut off from people. However, it is actually harder to deal with numerous traumatic events because the stress piles up over time. Going through numerous traumatic events takes more of a toll on your body and your coping abilities, making it really important for you to deal with what has affected you.

How you react to trauma depends not only on the social support available to you, but also on your age when the event or events happened (Brewin, Andrews, and Valentine 2000). If you were very young, you may not have had the verbal skills needed to even describe what happened to you. Instead, maybe you were afraid of strangers, had trouble sleeping, or were irritable or aggressive. Young kids who are traumatized also may be "behind" their peers when it comes to milestones like walking, talking, or learning to read. Elementary school kids who have been traumatized often have difficulty trusting adults or other people their age. They also may not be able to talk about the trauma in a logical, orderly way. This doesn't mean they haven't experienced something terrible. In fact, the mind is not a video camera. If you've been traumatized as a kid, teen, or adult, it's perfectly normal for there to be things that are difficult to recall. During times of trauma, the brain doesn't process information like it does on a normal day. Finally, by the time you are a teenager, you deal with trauma in many of the same ways an adult would. That might include impulsivity and aggression, harming yourself, anxiety or worry, difficulty concentrating, difficulty forming close friendships, sadness, substance use, appetite or sleep changes, or physical health problems.

In addition, not all kinds of trauma affect us in the same way. Traumas like natural disasters or motor vehicle accidents can be a little easier to recover from emotionally, because you might not feel that you were specifically targeted for something bad to happen to you. On the other hand, when someone you love is violent toward you either physically or sexually, that can be very difficult to deal with. These kinds of events make it hard for you to trust people close to you and might make you feel ashamed or unloved. No one ever deserves trauma to happen to them. As we talk about ways to heal, we will keep reminding you that no one deserves to be victimized, and everyone deserves love and respect.

If you've experienced traumatic events in your life, here are some specific things you may be experiencing (American Psychiatric Association 2013):

* *Having unwanted thoughts or feelings about the event(s).* This might include painful thoughts and images about the trauma, nightmares, a feeling of intense anxiety when you are reminded of the event, feeling out of touch with your body when you are reminded of the event, and strong body reactions—like your heart racing—when you are reminded of the trauma.

* *Avoiding things.* You might be avoiding thoughts about what happened to you, or you might try to avoid people or places that remind you of the event(s). While avoidance may work in the short term, in the long term, it can leave you feeling very lonely and limited. You might find that you spend so much time avoiding things that you are no longer doing things you once enjoyed.

* *Dealing with painful thoughts and emotions.* You might find that after the traumatic event(s), you have difficulty recalling what happened to you. You may feel that you are a bad person or that the world is a bad place, or you might blame other people for what happened to you. You might feel overwhelmed with trying to make sense of what you experienced. Maybe you are dealing with sadness, guilt, shame, fear, or anger. Additionally, you may feel that you

have difficulty forming close relationships, enjoy-ing activities, or experiencing positive emotions like love and joy.

* *Experiencing emotions that you cannot control.* This includes feeling irritable, becoming aggressive, doing things to hurt yourself, feeling on edge, having dif-ficulty concentrating, or having problems sleeping.

* *Feeling out of touch.* Some survivors of trauma some-times feel out of touch with their bodies or their surroundings.

Although these symptoms can feel scary and overwhelm-ing, it is important to remember that you are not crazy. You are having an understandable reaction to a very stressful event or events. In fact, your reaction makes you human. Getting support and learning coping skills can help you to deal with what you've lived through.

> *** Jaya Says *** *I have a friend who had experienced bullying on a few occasions for being "different," but she is very open with her friends and is really strong. One time, another incident of bullying occurred and she wasn't acting like her normal self. She would just respond with "fine" whenever we asked her how she was, though it was clear she wasn't really fine. Soon, she told us that this time, the bullying really had gotten to her and that she became overwhelmed.*

How to Use This Book

Over the next week, pay attention to the types of thoughts and feelings you are having. Using the lists above and the one below, try to sort out what you are experiencing.

* Are you dealing with a lot of unwanted thoughts or reminders of the trauma?

    * Please read chapters 2–5.

* Are you avoiding thoughts, feelings, people, and places?

    * Please read chapters 5–6 and 9.

* Do you have painful emotions, like guilt, shame, or a feeling of emotional numbness that keeps you from experiencing positive emotions like joy and love?

    * Please read chapters 2, 3, 6, 8, and 10.

* Do you have intense emotions you cannot control, like guilt, anger, or concentration problems?

    * Please read chapters 3, 7, and 9.

* Do you generally feel out of touch with yourself and your environment?

    * Please read chapters 4 and 9.

Putting It All Together

Remember that traumatic events are very common in our culture and that you are not alone. When stress is unexpected or very severe, it may be traumatic. Post-traumatic stress is an understandable set of reactions to very painful events. You may be experiencing unwanted memories, you might be avoiding people or places, or you might be struggling to deal with your emotions. Taking steps to reach out to others and to learn different ways of coping is extremely courageous. If you are not working with a therapist, consider reaching out to a trusted adult for support. This is particularly important if you have had thoughts about hurting yourself or anyone else. You should not deal with that alone. Think about teachers, guidance counselors, or other adults you feel might be helpful and kind, and ask them if they know about resources for teens who are coping with stress. You can also find help through the resources listed at the back of this book.

Our Final Thoughts

Don't forget that it takes unbelievable courage to face your problems. Give yourself a lot of credit for getting this far!

chapter 1

Trauma and Negative Coping

This book will ask you to challenge yourself, to try new ways of looking at things, and to practice things that might not come easily at first. But before that process, this chapter will help you look at how well you are taking care of yourself and how to develop some healthy coping strategies. It might seem obvious that trauma affects how you think and how you feel. What is less obvious is that trauma can affect your physical health. When you are worried, depressed, or feeling upset, your body becomes chronically stressed. Obviously, it is very difficult to live like that. In times of stress, some people turn to things like hobbies, friends, spirituality, or exercise. Others may cope by turning to alcohol, drugs, overeating, or even risky sex to make themselves feel better—at least for the moment.

When talking about coping methods, we will avoid labeling things as "good" or "bad." For example, while it is understandable that someone who isn't sleeping well after a traumatic event might turn to alcohol, that coping mechanism isn't likely to work well in the long term. It doesn't make them a bad person, but this coping strategy is unhealthy, especially in the long run. So we will use the terms "healthy" and "unhealthy" to discuss how you are taking care of yourself. If you can, try not to judge yourself harshly for the way you are coping. Just take an honest look at what you are doing and consider if it is healthy or unhealthy for your body over the long term. Traumatic events that happen to us as kids and as young adults can influence us for a lifetime. But the good news is that younger people are more likely to be able to stop unhealthy habits from building up and to start healthier ways of living. Compared to adults, teens are more likely to try new ways of dealing with situations and have fewer years of unhealthy habits. By starting now, you can literally change your destiny.

Because trauma often involves a violation of your body, you may find it very difficult to think of your body as worthy of care or respect. Particularly if you have been through multiple traumas, you may feel that you are not important, which might be one reason you'd turn to unhealthy coping mechanisms. But you are important. Each human being has a right to live with dignity, respect, and care from others. That includes you. You can start by showing yourself the care and respect you deserve. Before we talk about how to start healthy ways of coping, let's look at how you might be coping now. Remember, this isn't about judging yourself. It's about figuring out what you are doing now, knowing you are young enough to try new things and change your future.

Unhealthy Coping

Unhealthy coping mechanisms come in a variety of forms, from overuse of alcohol or drugs, to using food to soothe yourself, to engaging in risky sexual behavior. Let's look at these unhealthy coping mechanisms and see if you think you're using any of them to deal with your trauma.

Alcohol and Drugs

Alcohol and drug use is a common way that trauma survivors deal with unwanted memories or with difficulty sleeping. Drugs can include over-the-counter medications, prescription medications, or substances like nicotine, marijuana, cocaine, and heroin.

Anna: *"I know I'm drinking too much."* Anna, a sixteen-year-old high school junior, was sexually assaulted by a friend at a party. Because Anna did not have permission to go to the party, she never told her parents about what she'd endured. Anna thought her parents would blame her for the assault, and she felt ashamed and afraid of how her friends would react if they knew about what happened. The assailant was a very popular kid who did well in sports and was active in school clubs. Anna had considered the assailant a friend, which left her feeling even more betrayed.

She had nightmares almost every night about the assault. To cope with her feelings, she started to drink vodka from her parents' liquor cabinet without their knowledge. Over the course of a few months, Anna realized that she needed to *drink more and more vodka to get to sleep and that she was still waking up at night. She also had frequent headaches in the morning, and her schoolwork was suffering. Prior to the assault, Anna used to smoke cigarettes occasionally with her friends. After the assault, she started smoking almost half a pack a day. Smoking helped her feel less anxious, particularly on days when she was worried that she might see her attacker at school.*

Although Anna was coping as best as she could, alcohol and cigarettes will have serious long-term implications for her health, her grades, and even her relationships. Anna realized that she needed to talk to someone about what had happened to her because dealing with it by herself wasn't working.

Food

Some trauma survivors find that they cope with feelings of depression, loneliness, shame, and anxiety by using food. Binge eating, overeating, purging (using laxatives or vomiting), over-exercising, and overly restricting food intake are common in trauma survivors.

Megan: "I thought the past was behind me." Megan was neglected as a child. Her mother suffered from bipolar disorder and was not taking her medication regularly. Her father left the family when Megan was very young, leaving her and her two younger siblings alone with their mom. Megan's earliest memories, as early as age seven, are of having to cook meals for her siblings when her mother was not at home, sometimes for days at a time. At seven years old, she learned how to open cans, microwave food, and manage with the meager food supply they had in the house. Megan never told anyone what was going on at home because she was afraid that she and her siblings would be split up if people knew her mother wasn't taking good care of them.

When Megan was fourteen, her mother entered treatment for her bipolar disorder, and her symptoms improved. However, Megan still had difficulty trusting the adults around her, including her mom. She would find herself bingeing on food, particularly on fatty or salty foods like fries and ice cream. When she ate, the taste of the junk food make her feel better for a short time, and she felt less depressed, at least for those moments. After Megan gained forty pounds in one year, a concerned teacher, Ms. Weber, asked her what was happening at home. Although Megan did not confide in her at first, she eventually decided to talk to Ms. Weber, who encouraged Megan to talk to the high school counselor. Megan had assumed that the stress of her early childhood was behind her and hadn't realized that it was still affecting her so much.

Sometimes, it is clear that a traumatic event is causing you to cope in an unhealthy way. Using food as a way of coping might not be so obvious. In Megan's case, she did not immediately connect her eating patterns to her childhood trauma; she only knew that eating made her feel better, at least for a little while. Having a mentally ill caregiver, living in poverty, not having an adult you can count on, and being afraid of your family splitting up are long-term, toxic stressors that influenced Megan.

She was lucky to have a teacher who noticed her weight gain and who cared enough to refer her to a counselor. By recognizing her unhealthy coping, Megan can now take much better care of herself in the future to avoid potential health problems (like diabetes, which runs in her family) as an adult.

Risky Sexual Behavior

Another way that trauma survivors may cope is by engaging in high-risk sexual behavior, such as sex with multiple partners without condoms and sex without birth control. They may also find themselves in unstable relationships or relationships in which they are disrespected or treated poorly.

Richard: *"I'm just living for today." Seventeen-year-old Richard lived in a neighborhood filled with violence. Many of his classmates had witnessed or been the victim of a violent crime. He constantly worried about walking home from school safely. In fourth grade, Richard's classmate Eddie was shot by a stray bullet while he was outside playing basketball. Richard's home life didn't feel safe either. His mother and stepfather frequently screamed at each other, putting each other down and calling each other names.*

In high school, Richard started dating but had difficulty staying faithful to one person. He often thought, If I could die tomorrow, I might as well have fun. *But sometimes Richard felt guilty that he emotionally hurt girls he genuinely cared about. He also wondered if he would ever be able to feel close to anyone. Richard was recently diagnosed with chlamydia. Although the doctor told him this sexually transmitted disease was treatable with antibiotics, Richard was concerned when the doctor also said the disease might have long-term implications on his fertility.*

Richard's example shows that coping with trauma can be complex. If you don't feel safe at home or in your community, you might develop a sense of *foreshortened future,* which is the belief that you might not live past a certain age or that your future is limited. This feeling might cause you to make reckless decisions and to feel afraid of forming trusting relationships. In this case, Richard's doctor can play a key role in helping him change some of his behavior before it takes a long-term toll on his health.

Overall, these examples illustrate that unhealthy coping as a response to trauma can take many forms. When it comes to substance abuse, teens might be aware that they are using drugs (including nicotine) and alcohol to cope with what they've been through. However, unhealthy coping that involves food or sexual risk might be less obvious.

Try This! Identify How You Cope with Difficult Feelings

Not every kind of unhealthy coping is linked to trauma, but often, there are reasons behind why we don't respect our bodies: depression, anxiety, loneliness, or shame. Frequently, unhealthy coping is a way to deal with difficult feelings and traumatic events.

Over the next week, take an honest look at the way you are coping with difficult feelings. Ask yourself the following questions:

- *Am I using drugs (including nicotine) or alcohol to cope with my trauma?*

- *Do I use food (either through restricting, overeating, and so forth) as a way to cope with trauma?*

- *Do I engage in high-risk sexual behavior as a result of trauma?*

- *Are there other things I do because I don't think I'm worth it (for example, I drive recklessly, I never go the doctor, I deliberately hurt myself, I shop so much that I can't pay my bills)?*

One way to start looking at how you cope is to carry a notebook around with you to write down your habits for a week. Or you can record your behaviors on your phone or some other electronic device. However you decide to keep a log, make sure it is private and easy to access.

Once you have taken an honest look at how you are coping for about a week, you should think about healthier coping methods to replace unhealthy choices. Sometimes, you can find healthier strategies on your own. But there are definitely times when you will need more help.

If you are having a serious problem with drugs, alcohol, an eating disorder, or other very risky behavior, please don't try to tackle things all by yourself. Reach out to a trusted adult for help. That adult doesn't need to be someone close to you. For example, if there is a teacher in your school who you know has helped other people, reach out to him or her, even if you don't know the teacher directly. If you don't think you have anyone you can talk to, check out the resources listed at the back of this book. Trusting someone else with your story is courageous. It is brave. For many teens, it is essential. Please do not suffer alone.

Finding Your Strengths

Trauma doesn't need to define who you are or the person you will become. Although what you've experienced will always be a part of you, you also have strengths that are a part of you. *Post-traumatic growth* is a term that means that people who have survived something very difficult can become very brave, resourceful, and wise. Although no one would choose to have something extremely stressful happen to them, post-traumatic growth can be a positive side effect of experiencing trauma. *Resilience* is the ability to cope and thrive with life's challenges. It is a key part of post-traumatic growth.

> ✳ **Jaya Says** ✳ *To me, being resilient means that you can enjoy life more, you can recover when someone hurts you, and you can take what life throws at you. I see people who are resilient and brave enough to try new things, and that's something I admire. I'm trying hard to develop resilience in myself because it's a good life skill to have.*

Try This! What Makes You Unique

Identifying your strengths is the first step toward healing. It might be very difficult for you to do this, particularly if you struggle with feelings of shame and self-blame. Ask friends or family to list your best qualities. If you feel too awkward to ask them in person, send a text telling them you are working on a project and asking them to list three of your best attributes. Remember, we all have different strengths and weaknesses. The key to growth and healthy coping is learning to build on those strengths once we figure out what we are best at. Some people are very extroverted, always looking to make friends and connections. Others are very detailed-oriented and are good at researching solutions to problems. Still others are creative and have great imaginations. Everyone is different, and resilience looks different for everyone. As a way to identify your strengths, take a look at what statements describe you the most:

- *I reach out to others in times of stress.*

- *I get along with a lot of types of people.*

- *I consider myself a good judge of character.*

- *I use humor to help me cope.*

- *I am the kind of person who likes to read and research things.*

- *I like to make lists and set goals.*

- *I am organized when I am working toward a goal.*

- *I am a creative or "out-of-the-box" thinker.*

- *When no one is around to help me, I am good at coming up with ways to help myself.*

- *I have a great imagination.*

- *I am the kind of person who notices details.*

- *I like to focus on the big picture or the big goals.*

Now that you have thought about what your strengths are, you can better figure out what types of healthy coping methods are best for you. For example, if you are someone who has been drinking to deal with negative feelings but you notice details and have a great imagination, you might want to try art or music as a form of expression. If you have found yourself over-eating but you actually like connecting to others, maybe a support group (in person or online) would be helpful. If you love to research things, maybe you can make a list of how changing unhealthy habits will benefit you and carry the list with you to reread whenever you need inspiration. The important thing is to think about how your unique skills will help you find your own path. You are unique and will find a unique path to healing.

Healthy Coping

It is easy for people to tell you to stop doing things: stop smoking, drinking, eating too much, or having unprotected sex. But if it was that easy to do, no teen would ever struggle with these issues. And we know that teens do struggle with these issues—very often. When you have lived through something traumatic, you are using these methods to help cope with your feelings and symptoms. The key to changing these unhealthy behaviors is to figure out what you can replace them with.

Again, this is an individual path. One size doesn't fit all. The best way to figure out what works for you is to view things as an experiment. Try not to judge the technique too much. Just go in with an open mind, commit to trying out a new strategy for a week, and see how it works for you. Your teen years are filled with new experiences and learning about yourself, and this is one of those opportunities.

* Jaya Says * *For me, trying new things is difficult, and it takes a lot of courage for me to do something outside of my comfort zone. However, when I do try new things, I realize that sometimes I learn new things about myself that I didn't know before. Over one summer, I took an art class with people I didn't know in a place I'd never been before. As a result, I realized that I'm good at using pastels and charcoal, things I'd probably never know if I hadn't taken that class.*

Try This! Healthy Coping Strategies

If you are trying to reduce your unhealthy coping, you should also build up your healthy coping. Change doesn't happen all at once. Instead, successful change happens in small steps. Don't be discouraged if some days are healthier than others. When you are discouraged, think about what's called the "zero multiplication table": zero multiplied by anything is always zero, but even a fraction adds up over time. In the same way, if you make healthy changes, however small, you will see big changes over time. Here are a few healthy coping suggestions:

- Talk to friends about what is bothering you

- Try to have fun with your friends

- Watch a comedy movie

- Play a sport you enjoy

- Do yoga

- Pray

- Read a book that isn't related to schoolwork or trauma

- Do something creative

- Take a walk

- Play a game

When thinking about healthy coping, think about the strengths you have already identified. Maybe you are creative or social or a really organized thinker. Maybe you prefer to do things alone, or perhaps you love being a leader. Select one or two strategies to start with and try them out for a week or two. If they don't work well for you, keep trying until you find something that fits.

As you begin your journey toward healthy coping, you may find your-self thinking, *I don't feel like I'm worth it* or *I deserved what happened to me* or *I don't think I can change.* Discouraging thoughts like these are very common, particularly when you first begin trying healthier ways of coping. Jot down these thoughts when they come up to see how often they're affecting you. In order to try out healthier coping strategies, you have to be able to "talk back to" or "challenge" those thoughts. Here are some things you can tell yourself when these thoughts arise:

- *Everyone is worthy of love and respect.*

- *My body deserves care.*

- *Even though my coping methods aren't great, I can learn new skills.*

- *I am a good person, even though my coping methods aren't as healthy as I want them to be.*

- *I don't have to make changes all at once.*

- *Getting help means that I am courageous.*

Learning new ways of coping takes time and effort, but you can do it. The good news is that teens are in a unique position to change the course of their health—and their lives. You are still learning new things about yourself every day, so don't be afraid to try a new, healthy way of coping. It takes almost two months to learn a new habit. So, if you encounter bumps in the road, forgive yourself and keep going. And remind yourself that you have what it takes to practice new skills.

Putting It All Together

It is important to take an honest look at how you are coping, both healthily and unhealthily. Unhealthy coping mechanisms do not make you a bad person. They only make you human— someone who has lived through some very traumatic events. By starting new, healthy habits, you are setting yourself up for a healthier future both emotionally and physically. By taking care of yourself, you are declaring that you worthy of respect, from yourself and others.

Start paying attention to your strengths. Resilience is a skill that you can develop, and it starts with figuring out where your natural abilities are and going from there. Developing those strengths is important as you begin to tackle some very difficult symptoms, including dealing with distressing trauma-related thoughts and feelings, which is the focus of the next chapter.

Our Final Thoughts

Remember that you have done the best you can to cope with what you've been through. And remind yourself that finding healthy ways to cope is a great way to change the course of your life!

chapter 2

Why Can't I Forget?

One of the most common reactions to trauma is wanting to forget about it and move on with your life. You may have experienced other people telling you to move on, and maybe you are mad at yourself for being unable to do so. If you feel like this, don't be too hard on yourself. This chapter will teach you about trauma and memory, offering you some suggestions about how to better manage difficult memories. We will also encourage you to have patience and compassion toward yourself as you heal.

How the Brain Reacts to Trauma

Understanding what happened to your mind and body during the traumatic event(s) is an important step in being kinder to yourself. Without getting into lots of technical details, let's look at how your physiology changes during a traumatic event. The *amygdala* is one part of the brain that responds when you are in a dangerous situation. It communicates with another part of the brain, the *hypothalamus,* which activates the *sympathetic nervous system* (SNS). The SNS gets your body physically ready for a threat by activating the fight-or-flight response. In other words, your body gets ready to run away or to fight the danger directly. At this point, you will feel your heart racing, your breathing is rapid, your pupils are dilated (for better vision), and your body secretes insulin to increase your energy level (Heim and Nemeroff 2009; Pace and Heim 2011; Yehuda 2009). After the danger has passed, your body relaxes and goes back to a normal state of functioning, called *homeostasis*.

Sometimes, when the danger is inescapable, our bodies might also respond with something called the *dissociative freeze response*. If you cannot run away and if you cannot fight, your body might try an alternative way to keep you safe at the time of trauma. This can involve becoming emotionally "numb" and freezing physically. Your body might release *analgesics*, naturally occurring chemicals in your body that help numb pain. During the freeze response, the body also reduces any movement (freezes), and your thoughts slow down. You might even have difficulty remembering the details of what actually happened to you (Briere, Scott, and Weathers 2005). This kind of freeze response is seen in both human and animals, especially when the danger is severe and inescapable. In a way, you are trying to "play dead" until the danger passes. As terrible as it sounds, the freeze response actually makes a lot of sense in traumatic situations (Raja 2016).

Regardless of whether you experienced fight, flight, or freeze when you were traumatized, it is clear that trauma isn't like other ordinary stressors. When you understand that your body has gone through a very complex process to fight for survival, you can appreciate that this isn't the same as dealing with daily stressors, like a bad grade or a misunderstanding with a friend. Basically, you are having a normal set of reactions to a very terrible set of events, and it is okay to take some time to heal.

Our Nonstop Culture

One thing that can get in the way of healing from trauma in our culture is that many people have a short attention span and expect others to move on from things quickly. These days, it is not uncommon to do multiple things at once, like talk, text, and send e-mail. Some people have multiple browsers open when working on something. Or when you are talking to a friend, you might be looking at your phone, wondering if someone has sent you a message. The average attention span is now approximately eight seconds, down several seconds from decades ago (Borreli 2015). That means it usually takes us just eight seconds before our mind jumps to a different idea.

What does this all have to do with trauma? Unfortunately, the mind and body do not just "get over" trauma quickly. It takes time to heal. But our fast-moving culture sets us up to (falsely) believe that people will get over traumatic things rapidly. We live in a culture where people don't always focus on other people's distress for a long period of time. That can be really painful, especially if you are trying to get support. However, that doesn't mean that you should give up. It means that you need to choose where you get your support wisely and that people need more education about trauma and post-traumatic stress disorder (PTSD). It also means that you need to be kind and patient with yourself as you heal.

> ✻ **Jaya Says** ✻ *Our nonstop culture is everywhere. My family is sometimes on electronics while I'm trying to have a conversation or vice versa. We need to take time to try to listen to each other. With my friends, I try to make an effort to give them my full attention when they want to talk about something, even if it isn't serious. Ignoring someone and what they have to say can come off as rude and hurt someone else.*

Luke: *"I have to live with what I did." Luke is a sixteen-year-old sophomore in high school. When he was twelve, he found his dad's gun in the dresser. Although his father had warned him never to play with it, Luke and his friends began to horse around with it, assuming it was unloaded. When Luke's little sister, Emily, walked in the room, she became frightened. He laughed and told her the gun wasn't loaded, and pulled the trigger. To Luke's horror, he shot his sister in the area around her right ear. He doesn't remember what happened immediately after the shooting or for several days afterward. The family was fortunate because Emily survived the shooting, although she required multiple surgeries on her ear and became partially deaf as a result of the shooting.*

Over the years, friends and family told Luke that what happened wasn't his fault, but Luke suffered from terrible periods of depression and anxiety. He felt incredibly guilty, wondering if Emily's life would have been better if he were never born. At the age of fourteen, he began skipping school and drinking beer with a few older boys who had dropped out of high school. By age sixteen, he was on academic probation and had been arrested several times for stealing from a local store. His parents would tell him that his behavior was unacceptable and criminal, and the judge told him that if he was caught stealing again, he would be sent to juvenile hall.

Sadly, Luke's case suggests that we are not always aware of how trauma influences people. His inability to remember what happened in the days after the shooting makes sense when we consider the fight, flight, or traumatic freeze response his body underwent during the accident. Luke himself didn't realize that the guilt he had about shooting his sister influenced his drinking, which then led to problems in school and with the law. His parents and the juvenile justice system also didn't recognize the connection. Instead, well-meaning people expected that Luke would "get over" his trauma relatively quickly. Luke's story also shows us that you don't always have to be the victim of a crime to be traumatized. While he made a grave mistake, the fact that his parents neglected to keep his environment safe also contributed significantly to his tragedy.

* **Jaya Says** * *There was an incident of serious bullying at my school once, and I couldn't help but see the bully as a horrible and mean person. However, I found out this person's story, and I realized this girl was going through so much at home. Students (myself included) saw this girl as a horrible person, yet we had no idea what was going on at home. Sometimes, the "bad" kids are struggling and aren't actually "bad."*

Finding Supportive People

Finding help is a key part of healing from trauma and PTSD. Almost no one can do this all by themselves. Finding someone you trust, preferably an adult, can be very helpful. If there are no adults you can turn to, trying to find a friend you can turn to can also help a lot. You might be wondering how you can figure out if someone is trustworthy. After all, trauma often involves someone betraying your trust and hurting you. But there are ways you can try to figure out who you can trust.

* **Jaya Says** * *I once had a friend pull me aside after school, then she told me she was bisexual. She also told me that I was the first person to know. I was very honored and grateful that my friend trusted me enough to know that I wouldn't judge her or make fun of her. I know how important it is to have trusted people you can open up to, without judgment.*

Try This! Identify Your Support Circles

Draw three large circles on a piece of paper and label them ACQUAINTANCES, REGULAR FRIENDS, and TRUSTED FRIENDS.

- In the first circle, write down the names of all of your acquaintances. These should be people with whom you enjoy spending time. They don't have to know too much about you, but they should generally be respectful of you. You probably don't make an effort to spend extra time with acquaintances, but if they are in your classes or activities, you don't mind talking with them.

- In the next circle, write down the names of friends. This circle should include people you enjoy seeing outside of regularly scheduled activities. You make an effort to spend time with them, and they like spending time with you. For example, a friend might send you a text on a weekend to say hello, or you might decide to hang out together at a basketball game. People in this category don't need to know everything that you've experienced. You generally enjoy their company, but you don't always know too much about each other's personal history. These people are likely to help you out with day-to-day tasks (like forgetting an assignment at school), but you probably don't rely on them for emotional support.

- In the final circle, write down the names of people you trust. These are people who might know something about your personal history, although they might not know that you are a trauma survivor. They allow you to express yourself emotionally, and you can rely on them to help you out from time to time. They might also share their feelings with you, so the relationship is a two-way street. In this circle, you might have some people your age, but you might also have some adults.

As you look at the third list, ask yourself what makes someone worthy of your trust. Someone who is generally kind to others? Someone you've seen helping others with their problems? Someone who has opened up to you about something personal? Your trauma history is personal. Before you decide whom to share it with, you get to decide if they're worthy. That can be based, in part, on how they have treated you in the past, how they have treated others in distress, and how open they have been with you. Ideally, you want at least a few people on your trusted list (and remember that you can also find more support through the resources listed at the back of this book). In the end, it doesn't matter how you find people you can trust, it only matters that you have them there to help you on your journey.

Being Patient with Yourself

In addition to having support, a big part of healing is learning that trauma may not follow a set timeline. If you find yourself wishing that you could just get over your trauma or telling yourself that you should no longer be dwelling on it, there is a two-part technique that can help. The first part involves recognizing your *should-statements*—that is, figuring out when you are ordering yourself to do something impossible or judging yourself too harshly. The second part involves *reframing* those thoughts into something that is healthier for you.

> **✱ Jaya Says ✱** *When I'm trying to reframe my thoughts or change my mind-set, I'm often hard on myself, as if I'm doing it for a grade or I'm going to have to write a report on it that's due the next day. I have to remind myself that this isn't school and that nothing's going to be perfectly dealt with in one day. It's hard for me to shake off that "school mind-set" sometimes.*

Try This! Identify the "Shoulds" and Reframe Them

Tomorrow, keep a tally of every time you use the word "should" in relation to your trauma. Some examples of should-statements include:

- *I should be over this by now.*

- *I should have known better.*

- *I should not need help.*

- *I should be doing better, but I'm not.*

- *I should be able to talk about it without breaking down.*

- *I shouldn't talk about what happened to me.*

- *I shouldn't upset others by talking about what happened to me.*

- *I shouldn't be so anxious/depressed/worried all of the time.*

Once you've kept a tally, write down the most common should-statements you use. Try to determine if there are any common themes to your statements. For example, are they about how you should or should not express yourself emotionally? Are they about how much you should or should not think about your trauma? Are they about how long you should or should not be upset by things that have happened?

The next step is to *reframe* some of your should-statements—trying to look at a thought in a different way, seeing if there is an alternate view of the same situation. First of all, you have to ask yourself if your thought is completely true. Does your thought look at both sides of the issue? Thoughts that you can reframe usually have key words that you can pick out pretty easily, words like "always," "never," "everyone," and "no one." For instance, *I **should** be over being bullied by now. **Everyone** says so.* Or, *I **shouldn't*** *upset people by talking about my rape. I'll **never** get over this.* When you find yourself making such general statements, see if you can reframe them. Here are some examples to get you started:

- *I should be over this by now. Anyone else would be dealing with this better than I am.* → *Healing normally takes time.*

- *I should be able to talk about it without breaking down. I'll never be normal.* → *I can learn ways to deal with my feelings in small, manageable steps.*

- *I shouldn't be so anxious all the time. Everyone thinks I'm crazy.* → *The way we react to trauma isn't just like regular stress, so I am doing the best I can.*

Coming up with one or two reframing statements and using them often can be a useful strategy. Write these statements down on paper or keep them accessible on your phone. The goal is to try to catch some of your should-statements and replace them with healthier, more balanced thoughts. If you are having trouble coming up with reframing statements on your own, see if someone you trust can help you.

Acceptance

In addition to reframing some of your thoughts, you can also work on accepting what has happened to you. First, it's important to define the word "acceptance." In this case, acceptance doesn't mean that you like what happened to you. It doesn't mean that you wanted it to happen, and it certainly doesn't mean that you would want to ever live through it again. Instead, acceptance means that you eventually come to an understanding that the trauma—maybe an assault, an accident, ongoing violence, a sudden loss or illness—isn't something you can change. None of us can change the past. However, your past does not have to dictate what happens in your future. In some ways, teenagers have an advantage here. You still have many years ahead of you to try new things and create a new story for your life.

> **✱ Jaya Says ✱** *I have a friend I admire because she is known for being optimistic. Yet, somehow, she's still a realistic person. When something goes wrong, she acknowledges it and decides to keep going. This is something I want to work on, because optimism isn't necessarily my strongest trait, and I know it's a helpful skill for myself and in life in general.*

Try This! Create a Metaphor

As you start your journey toward healing, you might have days when you don't think you can do it. The past might feel overwhelming. One way to motivate yourself to keep making progress is to create your own personalized metaphor for change and then do something special to remember it.

How can you create a metaphor? First, choose something that represents your healing journey—maybe a river filled with strong currents and lots of rocks, or a racecourse with hurdles and climbing walls. Next, visualize how you will overcome those obstacles—perhaps by navigating the rocky river in a strong boat with a sense of commitment, or running the race in your best gym shoes with your friends cheering you on. Your change metaphor can be anything that has meaning for you. Choose something that challenges you, but something you can imagine conquering. Visualize how strong and brave you feel during your journey, and how much stronger and braver you'll feel still when you have reached your goal.

Once you've chosen your own personal change metaphor, find a way to express it that is meaningful to you. Some suggestions include:

- Write it down in the form of a story or poem

- Paint or draw your metaphor visually

- Create video images or save pictures that remind you of the metaphor

Your metaphor is a tool to stay motivated during times when you might feel frustrated or overwhelmed. The metaphor will remind you that healing isn't easy, but that you have the strength it takes to get there.

Putting It All Together

Our brains are not wired to forget trauma easily. Unfortunately, people around us (and we ourselves) sometimes expect that we should be able to heal quickly. To heal from trauma, you need support and you need to give yourself the time that is needed. Learning to reframe thoughts that place an unrealistic expectation on you (such as, *I should be over this by now*) is a way to be kinder to yourself. Using a change metaphor can also help you when you are feeling overwhelmed and frustrated.

Our Final Thoughts

None of us can change the past. Give yourself the gift of patience and support as you create a brighter future for yourself.

chapter 3

Why Me?

A common question that traumatized teens ask themselves is *Why?* You might have asked yourself, *How could this happen? What did I do wrong? Why did this happen to me?* There are no easy answers to these questions, but you should know that no one deserves to be traumatized. This chapter will help you take an honest look at what you have experienced while focusing on how you can feel safe in the present moment.

Trauma and Your Core Beliefs

Depending on how old you were when you were first traumatized, it is likely that what happened to you changed your view of the world. We all have *core beliefs*—basic ideas about how we think the world works and how people should behave. Maybe we believe that good things happen to good people, that hard work is always rewarded, or that things happen for a reason. Trauma shatters many of our core beliefs about the world. It is as if you have a mirror that has been cracked, and you need to figure out how to see the world again.

When our core beliefs have been disrupted, it is not uncommon for us to swing our beliefs in the totally opposite direction, like a pendulum. Some examples:

* *The world is a safe place.* → *The world is completely unsafe and scary.*

* *Good things happen to good people.* → *I must have done something to deserve this.*

* *By acting a certain way, you can control what happens to you.* → *I don't have control over anything.*

These examples illustrate certain *cognitive errors,* or ways of thinking that might be unhealthy for us, particularly after trauma. Learning to *challenge* our thoughts—meaning gently finding other ways to look at a situation—can be a very helpful strategy. We all spend a great deal of time "in our own minds" talking to ourselves. We might as well try to make that dialogue healthy and supportive of ourselves! Here are some common cognitive errors associated with trauma and ways to challenge them (Burns 1999).

All-or-Nothing Thinking

This form of thinking involves seeing things in absolute terms, as 100 percent true or untrue, and doesn't leave room for uncertainty. You know you are using all-or-nothing thinking (also called "black-and-white thinking") when you use words like "always," "never," "everyone," and "no one." For example, *Everyone blames me for being raped.* Is that true? Do you have evidence that every single person feels that way? A more accurate statement might be: *Some people will blame me for drinking before I was raped. But other people will understand that I didn't ask for it.*

Catastrophizing

This involves starting with something that is bothering you or worrying you, then assuming the worst possible outcome. Obviously, if you have been traumatized, it's very understandable that you may be thinking about the worst-case scenario. For example, *If I don't learn to deal with my symptoms, I am going to flunk out of school and I'll never amount to anything.* A more balanced approach is: *I will work on dealing with my symptoms. I am going to take one day at a time and not focus on things that haven't happened yet.*

Overgeneralizing

This is the tendency to take one incident and assume that it applies across circumstances and people. For example, *My teacher was impatient with me. She must hate the work I've been doing and think I'm worthless.* Trauma survivors may be prone to overgeneralization, especially when they aren't sure if they trust someone. It is a way of trying to keep yourself safe, but it also stops you from developing trusting relationships with people. A more accurate statement might be: *Maybe my teacher was having a bad day or my assignment wasn't on target. Let me see how she reacts tomorrow before I decide what to do.*

Jumping to Conclusions

This involves deciding that you know the outcome of a situation ahead of time. For trauma survivors, it is not uncommon to assume that you understand someone else's motivation or emotions, when you may not. For example, *I know the reason that they didn't ask me to hang out is that they think I'm damaged and weird. Even if I asked to join them, they would say no.* A healthier thought would be: *I'm not sure why they didn't ask me to hang out. I won't know until I ask them if I can join in.*

Personalizing

Many trauma survivors are quick to feel that things are their fault. They might think, for example, *My parents are fighting again; it must be because I upset them again* or *I know he hit me again, but that's only because I asked for it.* Personalization is related to the guilt and self-blame that so many trauma survivors feel. A more balanced viewpoint would be: *I am not responsible for how another person chooses to deal with their difficult feelings.*

Labeling

This cognitive error is closely related to personalizing and overgeneralizing. Instead of describing a behavior—yours or someone else's—you may be tempted to describe their character. For instance, *He cut me off in traffic. He's a jerk.* Or, *I cheated on my boyfriend. I'm a disgusting person.* While it is tempting to make broad statements, we are better off describing the situation and figuring out how to manage it differently. This doesn't mean that you should make excuses for people treating you badly. It is not okay for someone to demean you, disrespect you, or harm you physically. However, in these situations, another way to view the situation may help you to feel calmer. For example, *I have no idea why he drives like that. Thank goodness I'm okay.* If you are labeling yourself, learning a different way to talk to yourself doesn't mean it's okay to hurt others. To take the above example, a healthy thought might be: *I should take an honest look at why I cheated on my boyfriend and figure out what I need to do next. I am not a horrible person, even though I'm not proud of my actions.*

> ✳ **Jaya Says** ✳ *I often look at other people and think,* Oh, they wouldn't like me. *I've been in situations where I assumed too many things about others, and it turned out I was wrong. I know that I need to try to stop doubting myself around others. Negative thoughts like these can creep up easily, but I try to notice them and correct them. Doing this helps me to stop assuming things and sometimes gives me the courage to talk to the people I'm thinking about.*

Try This! Spot the Error

As a way to practice healthier thinking patterns, try to identify the kinds of errors contained in the statements below. Then see if you can rephrase some of these common things that teen trauma survivors say.

- *Because I am a good person, this shouldn't have happened to me.*

- *This happened to me because I am a bad person.*

- *No one will ever love me again.*

- *I am a horrible person for acting the way that I do.*

- *Because I can't concentrate, I am probably going to fail out of high school.*

- *People are going to see me as damaged.*

Overall, you can see plenty of all-or-nothing thinking, catastrophizing, overgeneralizing, jumping to conclusions, personalizing, and labeling in these statements. It is also easy to understand why you might start thinking this way when you've been through something very painful. So although we call these thinking patterns cognitive "errors," be kind to yourself when you are coming up with alternatives. With some practice, you will find that this kind of thinking can lose its power over you.

Keeping Yourself Safe

Guilt is regret for certain things you might have done in your life. It is not uncommon for trauma survivors to struggle with guilt. *Shame* is the sense that you are somehow defective or not worthy of love and happiness. If you feel guilty about something, you can figure out what you can do differently in the future. Shame, on the other hand, will not help you to stay safe in the future because you will see yourself as unworthy of love and care.

> Kara: *"I deserved what happened to me."* Kara, a senior
> in high school, had been dating her boyfriend since their
> sophomore year. Prior to graduation, Kara began to have
> doubts about their relationship. She had never dated other boys
> and was curious to meet other people. When Kara was visiting
> a friend who was in college, she had several shots of vodka
> and doesn't remember much about what happened next. When
> she woke up the next day, she was in a strange bedroom and
> realized that she had been raped. Kara never told anyone about
> what had happened to her.
>
> Over the next few months, she became convinced that she
> had "asked for" what had happened to her. She felt like she had
> betrayed her boyfriend and that she wasn't worthy of anyone's
> love or forgiveness. At times, she would cut herself. After a
> trusted teacher asked her about the marks on her arms, Kara
> opened up to her about what had happened. Together, they
> made an appointment to see the school social worker.

What Kara experienced is sadly common. Just because she was drinking as a teenager, it does not mean that she deserved to be victimized. In fact, being unconscious during her assault means that she could not have consented to having sex. Guilt is about changing the things you can control to try to keep yourself safer and healthier in the future. Shame doesn't help your recovery. Shame is very difficult to conquer on your own, and you almost always need someone you trust to help you out of it.

Try This! Keeping Yourself Safe

We know that no teenager or adult is perfect. We all make mistakes, and the important thing is being able to learn from them. Think about a time when you made a risky decision. Maybe you were impulsive in some way or did something you're not proud of. Consider the following:

- What was happening before you made this decision? What were you feeling? What thoughts were going through your mind?

- When you were in the situation, did you regret your actions immediately, or only afterward?

- How did you feel afterward? Did you have guilt about what you could have done differently, or was it shame about who you are as a person?

One way to deal with shame-inducing thoughts is to do something to show yourself that they do not represent who you are. These thoughts might include:

- *I am a terrible person.*

- *I deserved what happened to me.*

- *I am not worthy of respect.*

- *I hate myself.*

- *I didn't deserve to survive.*

Consider writing such thoughts down on a piece of paper, then putting the paper into a sink full of water. As you watch the words disappear and the paper fall apart, remember that you cannot base your idea of who you are on just one circumstance.

Dealing with Victim Blaming

As you work on recognizing your thinking patterns and staying healthy, you should also watch out for *victim blaming* in the environment—that is, partially or totally putting the blame on the person who was victimized, instead of on the person or the circumstance that did the hurting. Victim blaming is a way for people to emotionally distance themselves from events and victims, giving them a sense that traumatic events could never affect them. Unfortunately, victim blaming can be common, depending on the type of trauma. Victims of sexual abuse and domestic violence may feel particularly vulnerable to people judging them. One reason it is so common is that trauma threatens everyone. Although we would like the world to be 100 percent safe and predictable, we know that it doesn't always work that way.

When other people feel vulnerable to trauma, they may actually cope with it by trying to distance themselves from what happened to someone else, either by saying it could never happen to them or by claiming that it wasn't that big of a deal. Examples of this would be blaming the victims of sexual assault for wearing short skirts or asking people why they didn't leave their abusers sooner. Basically, victim blaming is a way for someone to cope with feeling overwhelmed about what happened. That doesn't make it right.

We have come a long way in understanding that no one deserves to be victimized. But we still need to educate people. As you feel your symptoms improve, one way to deal with victim blaming is to get active in your community. We will talk about this more in the discussion on resilience in chapter 10.

> **✳ Jaya Says ✳** *We live in a world where people like to judge others. Some take one glance at a person and decide they have them and their situation all figured out. I have classmates who learn about abusive relationships in health class, and they'll say, "Well, just leave the abuser!" The teacher will end up having to explain that it isn't that simple. The other kids are well-meaning, but they don't always understand how complicated the situation can be.*

Putting It All Together

One of the most difficult questions to answer is: *Why did this happen to me?* Often, there is not an adequate answer to that question. By exploring your thinking patterns, you can try to look at situations in a more balanced way. That is challenging, but it's very important to do after a traumatic event. Additionally, watching out for shame is essential for healing. You are someone who is worthy of love and respect. Chapters 6 and 10 will provide more insights on these topics.

Our Final Thoughts

No one is ever to blame for being victimized. While is it normal to ask *Why me?*, try to remember that there is a lot more that makes you unique than these particular struggles. You are a special person with something unique to contribute to the world.

chapter 4

Unwanted Thoughts, Nightmares, and Flashbacks

Have you ever been going about your day only to have something remind you of the traumatic event(s) you've been through? Maybe it is a certain place that cues a terrible memory. Maybe it is the look on a stranger's face or the smell of someone's perfume or cologne. Perhaps it is a certain sensation or a noise that takes you right back to something terrifying. These types of reminders are called *triggers,* and you might feel like they have a lot of power over you. As much as you try to avoid your triggers, you may sometimes find that you are still overwhelmed with unwanted memories. This chapter is focused on how to deal with unwanted thoughts of the trauma, nightmares, and flashbacks. Before we talk about how to deal with them, let's understand more about what they are and why you might be experiencing them.

Unwanted Thoughts

Perhaps you have worked very hard to avoid people or places that remind you of your trauma. Maybe you avoid going to certain places or being around certain kinds of people, or limit the types of things you do. And then, suddenly, in the middle of school or during an activity or while you are talking to a friend, a painful memory completely disrupts what you are doing. These memories can leave you in tears or so anxious that you cannot concentrate. Maybe you feel depressed for the rest of the day.

Ellen: *"Why I am still thinking about the abuse?" Ellen, a nineteen-year-old freshman in college, dated her high school boyfriend for the last three years of high school. At the beginning of their relationship, Jason was attentive and caring. But over time, he became verbally abusive, telling Ellen that she was ugly and that no one would ever love her. After about a year of dating, Jason would hit her when he became angry and apologize profusely afterward. On other occasions, he blamed Ellen for "making him" get so angry by flirting with other boys. Ellen didn't tell anyone because she was ashamed and believed that Jason might have a point; perhaps she was partially at fault for the abuse.*

Their relationship ended when Ellen went to an out-of-state college. She assumed she would be able to put the past behind her and make a new start. However, she sometimes found that when she was trying to study, she would have vivid recollections of Jason yelling at her and hitting her. Sometimes these memories were triggered by an unknown boy sitting next to her in class. At other times, she wasn't sure what brought on the painful thoughts. Ellen began to seriously worry about how her grades would be affected by these symptoms.

Ellen's story illustrates that you cannot always forget about the past. Although getting some distance between her and her boyfriend was certainly helpful, it was not enough to allow her to heal from this experience. Also, the fact that Ellen wasn't always able to predict her own triggers is common. In order to pass her classes and be able to develop healthy future relationships, Ellen will have to learn ways to manage her unwanted thoughts.

> **✳ Jaya Says ✳** *Most of my friends don't know much about dating violence, as it isn't talked about as much in school as other types of violence. Even though they understand what it is, most of them see it as something that could never happen to them. The truth is that anything can happen to anybody, even if we try to tell ourselves we're "too smart" or "too good" for something to happen to us.*

One of the ways that we can cope with difficult thoughts is by learning how to "talk to ourselves" about them. All of us talk to ourselves in our minds. In fact, if we count up all the things we say to ourselves in a day's time, we talk to ourselves more than anyone else talks to us! Learning kinder, more balanced ways of talking to ourselves can help when we are experiencing unwanted thoughts.

Try This! Refocus Your Thoughts

One of the most common reasons that unwanted thoughts spiral out of control is that we assume they are abnormal. However, unwanted thoughts are the brain's way of trying to protect us from future trauma. Basically, your brain is trying to process the terrible things you've been through to see if there are clues about how to stop them from happening again. Through no fault of your own, you may be making your unwanted, trauma-related thoughts worse by how you follow up these thoughts—meaning what you say to yourself next. For example, an unwanted thought or scary memory about your trauma might be followed with some of these thoughts:

- *I am going crazy.*

- *I will never get over this.*

- *I will never be normal again.*

- *I will never be able to stop thinking about this.*

- *I have to do something to stop dwelling on this.*

- *I need to make these thoughts stop.*

- *I shouldn't be thinking about this anymore.*

If any of these thoughts are common for you, one technique you can try involves learning to replace these thoughts with kinder, more nurturing responses. Sometimes, thoughts are like dominos, and if we can interrupt the chain, we can stop them from cascading and becoming even worse. To stop the cascade, think about how you might respond to a friend who has gone through what you have. Or what you would want a kind adult to say to you. Here are some suggestions:

- *Just because I have some thoughts about what happened to me, it doesn't make me crazy.*

- *What happened to me was terrible, but it doesn't define who I am.*

- *Anyone who went through what I did would think about it sometimes. I am normal.*

- *I am having an understandable reaction to a very terrible experience.*

- *I am not going to avoid my thoughts about this. Running away from my thoughts doesn't work. Facing my thoughts is brave.*

- *I know thinking about this is normal, and in time, I will be able to deal with things.*

It will take a lot of practice to learn these new ways of thinking. You might want to generate your own list. Depending on what works for you, you can write down the list of your refocused thoughts, video-record yourself saying these things, or even do something creative to reinforce them, like create a painting using words or illustrations of these more nurturing thoughts. However you do this, just make sure to refer back to your list often and keep it in a place where you will see it frequently. It will take a while for these nurturing thoughts to become second nature. But remember, nurturing thoughts can help stop unwanted thoughts from turning into hours of emotional difficulty.

Flashbacks

Flashbacks are similar to unwanted thoughts, but they are often much more intense. Perhaps a certain sight, sound, touch, or smell makes you feel that you are reliving the traumatic event all over again. During a flashback, you may feel confused about where you are and actually believe that your life (or someone else's) might be in danger. Perhaps you start shaking and sweating or your heart races. Flashbacks can be very scary. Some people may think that having a flashback means that they're going crazy. This isn't true. It just means that your mind is trying to process something extremely painful. Techniques that help you stay connected to your present environment can help you manage flashbacks.

> Asha: *"I just want to be left alone." Asha, a thirteen-year-old seventh grader, was the victim of bullying because of her weight. She had gained about twenty-five pounds after her parents divorced two years earlier. Asha felt that her mother loved her little brother more and that the only time her mother paid attention was to yell at her to "eat healthy food." Most of the bullying was in the school locker room, where kids would regularly tell Asha, "Go kill yourself." On a few occasions, the bullying was physical, with the kids throwing things at her.*
>
> *Even when she was at home, in a relatively safe situation, she found that people talking with raised voices caused her to shake and sweat. When violent scenes were on the television, she would become so anxious and sick to her stomach that she would forget where she was, feeling like she was back in school, being bullied. Her mind would be racing with thoughts like, I have to get out of here before someone hurts me. These flashbacks, in which Asha felt she was reliving the bullying, happened several times a week.*

Asha's case is very difficult because her bullying was ongoing, not a onetime event. One of the most important things she did was to reach out to a teacher for help. This teacher took Asha's bullying very seriously, and addressed it with the administration. Although the verbal bullying never completely stopped, the children did not physically harm her once the teachers became aware that this was going on. In addition, Asha worked with the school counselor to learn techniques to feel safer during her flashback episodes. The school social worker also helped her talk to her mother, who didn't realize how bad the bullying had gotten. Her mother became more supportive after the social worker gave her some suggestions about how she could help.

✳ **Jaya Says** ✳ *Most of my classmates see bullying as something bad, but not something that could happen to them. The truth is, it can happen to anybody. I think the worst part about being bullied is that you don't feel safe, and you might feel like there's nobody who can help you. When someone I know is bullied, I try to be there for them and make them feel less alone. Nobody is truly alone.*

One way to cope with flashbacks is to use *grounding techniques,* which are ways to remind yourself where you are and that you are safe. Grounding techniques rely heavily on using your senses. Anything that helps you remember where you are, who you are with, or keeps you connected to your environment can be used to cope with flashbacks.

Try This! Engage Your Senses

Flashbacks can leave you feeling very anxious, with your thoughts racing and your body in high gear (shaking, sweating, breathing hard). One way to deal with flashbacks is to plan ahead to figure what you can do when you feel yourself being triggered. Consider which one of your senses you would like to engage. Are you someone who likes to smell a nice candle? When you eat, do you really like the tastes of certain foods? Or when you listen to the sounds in the room, can you drown out all the other distractions? To use these techniques during an actual flashback, it is good to practice them daily, when you are not anxious. Here are some suggestions for grounding techniques. Remember, when you feel triggered and the anxiety begins to build, take a deep breath and choose one of your five senses to focus on.

Sight: Look at what is around you. If you are indoors, notice the color of the walls. If you are outdoors, pay attention to the color of the sky. Try to name the colors you see. Pay attention to the shapes. Describe the lighting. Is it soft, harsh? Are various objects lit differently? Keep breathing as you stay focused on what is around you, remembering where you are right now.

Sound: Listen to the sounds around you. Is it noisy or quiet? Can you hear cars or airplanes in the distance? Are there people around you? Is there the hum of a heater or air conditioner? Play your favorite song and focus on the melody and the harmony of the words and the instruments. As you attend to the sounds around you, remind yourself that you are now in a safe place.

Touch: Take a minute to feel your favorite soft blanket or stuffed animal. What does it feel like on your skin? Or run your hands over a smooth shell that you keep with you. Feel the difference between the jagged edges and the rippled outside of the shell. Perhaps you choose to take your shoes and socks off, and just pay attention to how your feet feel on the floor. Notice the sensations of your toes and heels. Remind yourself that whatever you are touching is right in front of you, keeping you connected to the present moment.

Smell: Consider keeping your favorite scented candle or a small bottle of your favorite perfume or aromatherapy oil with you. Notice how the scent makes you feel. Choose something that helps you feel safe and calm. As you inhale deeply, remind yourself that this scent is keeping you focused on what is happening right now, not what has happened in the past.

Taste: Keep your favorite mints or gum with you at all times. When you chew the gum or eat the mint, really pay attention to the taste. How long does the initial sweetness last? What is the feeling it produces when you chew it? Can you smell it? Use this as a way to stay with the current feeling and keep connected to your environment.

Grounding skills will take a while to master. It's important to practice them often, especially during times when you feel calm. That will make it more likely that you can use these techniques when you really need them. If your flashbacks are very intense and you lose large periods of time or become physically ill during them, please do not try to get better on your own. A trained mental health professional can help you learn these techniques and provide much-needed support. Reach out to a trusted adult for help or refer to the resources at the back of this book for ideas about where to find more help.

Nightmares

One of the worst symptoms of PTSD is nightmares. They can be terrible to live with. If you are not getting enough rest and if you are afraid to go to sleep, your waking hours become very challenging. When you aren't sleeping, it becomes extremely difficult to concentrate on schoolwork, you might lack the motivation to make friends, or you might be too tired to take good care of yourself. Sleep is essential for healthy brain development, especially in your teen years. You need sleep to learn, to concentrate, and to enjoy life. You might think you have no control over your sleep. The good news is that there are some techniques you can use that can help.

> Hailey: *"I should have done more for my friend."* Hailey is a fourteen-year-old girl. Her friend Ella took her own life over the summer. Ella had been struggling with depression, her parents had recently been through a nasty divorce, and the kids at school often told her she was fat. When she found out about Ella's death, Hailey was in shock. She blamed herself for not being a better friend and not knowing that this might happen. Hailey's parents were sympathetic at first, but after a while, they started to tell her that *"Ella would have wanted you to move on with your life."* Hailey took this as a sign that she shouldn't talk about Ella anymore and that her reaction was not normal.
>
> About three months after Ella's suicide, Hailey began to have vivid nightmares about her friend's last minutes. She would dream that she would find Ella dying but was unable to save her. Hailey would wake up with her heart racing. Sometimes, she would cry and not be able to get back to sleep.

The suicide of a loved one can be a very confusing and tragic event. It often leaves survivors feeling guilty about the things they wish they had done to prevent it. Hailey's parents meant well by encouraging her to move on with her life, but sometimes, this can backfire. In this case, Hailey could no longer share her feelings and emotions about her friend's suicide, and her sleep consequently became disrupted. Nightmares are a normal way to try to work out some of these difficult feelings.

Nightmares can be a difficult symptom, but there are some techniques that can help. You may find that you have the same (or similar) nightmare many times a week. You might be afraid to go to sleep or find it impossible to return to sleep once you've had the nightmare.

Try This! Caring for Your Sleep

It is normal to avoid thinking about the content of terrible dreams, but we are going to suggest that you allow yourself to think about these dreams—but find different endings. You do this by writing down your dream but ending it in a different way. This technique is called *imagery rehearsal.* So perhaps you have a dream in which someone is hurting you; you can choose to end it by seeing yourself in a safe, comfortable place, knowing that you are okay. Visualize what is around you. Maybe a soft blanket? A stuffed animal you love? Your beloved pet? You can create an ending where you feel safe. Practice writing down this ending every day. Alternately, you can videotape yourself talking about the different ending. The key is to commit to rehearsing this alternate ending *every single day* when you are awake and calm. The more you do that, the more you are training your mind, while it is awake, to end the dream differently. If you find this difficult to do on your own, you may want a therapist to help you.

Another thing you should do to help with your sleep is to make sure you have a sleep routine. This is also called *sleep hygiene,* which refers to the rituals that go along with sleep. We set the stage for a good night's sleep by what we do during the day and what we do in the hour before bed. Ask yourself the following questions:

- *Do I go to bed at the same time every night?*

- *Do I avoid the use of electronics one hour before bed?*

- *Is the place where I sleep free of electronic distractions (no cell phone, computer, and the like)?*

- *Do I avoid exercise one hour before bed?*

- *Do I get up at approximately the same time every day (within half an hour)?*

- *Do I avoid using naps to make up for lost sleep?*

For the best sleep, you should answer "yes" to most of these questions. The best sleep comes from a general routine, and irregular naps can definitely interfere with a good sleep schedule. Also, the noise and lights emitted from electronics can actually interfere with the natural rhythm of brain waves during sleep. Finally, the last hour before bed should be restful and include soothing activities, not strenuous exercise.

If you answered "no" to some of these questions, choose one area to work on every week. Make small changes and don't get discouraged if you aren't perfect. For example, try to move your phone to another room at night, so you aren't distracted by any buzzing in the middle of the night. However, if your phone makes you feel safe, start by moving the computer out of your room. The best way to reach these kinds of goals is to have a friend or family member who will support your progress. If you can, get someone you trust to help you work on a specific goal. For instance, "Mom, I am trying not to exercise after nine p.m. so I can go to sleep by ten thirty. In a few days, can you remember to ask me how I'm doing?" Staying accountable helps us to reach our goals. By keeping your goals small, you are more likely to experience success. You can always make your goals harder as time goes on.

Putting It All Together

Unwanted thoughts, flashbacks, and nightmares are some of the most difficult symptoms of PTSD. There are techniques that can help you manage these symptoms, including learning more nurturing ways to talk to yourself, practicing grounding techniques, and using imagery rehearsal and good sleep hygiene to combat nightmares. If your symptoms are causing you significant distress, you should seek professional help. For example, if you are missing days of school, if you are finding it impossible to concentrate, or if you are having thoughts about hurting yourself or others, please do not attempt to face things alone. There are trusted adults who want to help you heal—coaches, teachers, parents, friends, and others. Start by talking to someone or looking at the resources page of this book for further help.

Our Final Thoughts

Unwanted thoughts, flashbacks, and nightmares can be extremely scary. Experiment with grounding techniques that can help you, and don't be afraid to find someone who can support you emotionally. You don't have to face your fears alone.

chapter 5

Is My Fear Healthy?

When you have been through something traumatic, fear is one of the most common reactions. It can also be one of the most difficult, overwhelming, and isolating feelings. You are not alone. You are having a very understandable reaction to very difficult circumstances. This chapter will focus on how to deal with fear in small, manageable steps. Understanding how fear works is the first step in being able to manage it.

Immediately after a traumatic event or events, most people feel afraid. *Fear* usually refers to something specific. In the case of trauma, we might be fearful of a specific person (the perpetrator) or a certain place (the intersection where we were mugged). A certain amount of fear is a good thing. It helps to keep you safe. For example, if you never felt afraid, you might step into traffic without being worried about getting hit by a car. But over time, fear can turn into anxiety. *Anxiety* tends to be more general than fear and may or may not be focused on a specific source. Anxiety includes a general feeling of dread or worry that something bad may happen to you or others (Jantz and McMurray 2011). In addition, fear tends to become broader, or more generalized, with time. For instance, if you were hurt by an older man you know, your fear of the perpetrator can turn into a fear of all middle-aged men. Perhaps your fear of the street corner where you were mugged turns into a fear of any area outside of your block.

The most difficult thing about fear is that it can quickly take over your life. It can become bigger with time, and before you know it, you are avoiding all sorts of people and places that remind you of your trauma. What is even more difficult is that it becomes hard to judge what parts of your fear and anxiety are helping you to stay safe and what parts are harming you and limiting your life.

How Much Fear Is Too Much?

When something terrible has happened to you, you start to search for patterns—who did this, when did it happen, and where? By trying to figure out how and why traumatic events happen, your brain is trying to find ways to stop these events from happening again in the future (Janoff-Bulman 2010). In many ways, your brain is trying to protect you, focusing on your future well-being and safety. But in other ways, after a trauma, your brain's ability to calculate risk becomes impaired. Things that you once considered safe may suddenly feel overwhelming. This doesn't mean that something is wrong with you. It just means that you are reacting to trauma.

For example, if you have been sexually assaulted by a stranger, your immediate reaction might be to fear people you don't know. Over time, you might begin to question how well you know anyone and start to think that most people are untrustworthy. If your fear generalizes over time, you might become afraid of acquaintances and less likely to want to talk to people you do not know well. Although this is understandable, you can see how this kind of fear and anxiety might become very confining and leave you feeling very lonely. The result of avoidance is that you may find yourself becoming more and more limited in where you go and what you do.

So, how can you figure out how much fear is normal (for example, you should be afraid of someone who was actually violent toward you) and how much fear is unhealthy? One way to start is to think about all the things you may have wanted to do in the past week. Consider whether fear or anxiety got in the way of you doing what you wanted. Was this an activity you regularly engaged in before you experienced your trauma? Was this an activity you once thought was safe? Is this an activity that many of your peers do regularly? Sometimes, when we are overcome with fear, it's hard for us to judge a situation realistically. If you have a friend, family member, therapist, or other trusted adult in your life, ask them for their perspective on the situation.

Try This! Be a Reporter

One of the most challenging aspects of our fears is trying to figure out if they are realistic or not. One way to try to do this is to look at the people or places you are avoiding with some distance. Try to think of yourself as a reporter or lawyer. These people look at all sides of a situation, and they try to stick to the facts or things that can be proven. They ask challenging questions to come up with their conclusions. Think about a situation you are avoiding and ask yourself the following questions (but try to think like a reporter or a lawyer). Here are some questions you can ask yourself:

- *Is this a situation I used to participate in safely?*

- *How often have I participated in this situation safely?*

- *Do other people my age regularly participate in this situation safely?*

- *What evidence do I have that someone in this situation will harm me?*

- *Has someone in this situation harmed me before?*

- *Would I think this situation is safe for a friend?*

- *Is anxiety the main reason that I am avoiding this situation?*

- *Are there circumstances that would make this situation feel safe—for example, if I went with a friend?*

When you look at your answers, if you have safely participated in the situation in the past on numerous occasions, if others participate safely, if you have never been harmed in the situation, and if anxiety is the main reason you are avoiding the situation, you may want to consider facing your fear. Thinking about what circumstances will help you to face the situation will help you to break your goal into smaller steps, which will be useful in the next exercise.

Fear and the Teen Brain

Teenagers are in the process of growing and changing. We are learning more and more about how the teenage brain is different from the fully developed adult brain. For example, teens can often learn new information faster than adults. As a child, the gray matter in your brain (made up of connections of neurons or brain cells) increases at a rapid rate. In adolescence, the brain continues to connect networks of these neurons together, as you experience more in your life. Your learning speed increases, and your brain becomes better at recognizing patterns and synthesizing new information (National Institute of Mental Health 2011).

But teen brain development can also be challenging. Some (not all) teens experience periods of feeling overwhelmed by their emotions, and their judgment of a situation might be impaired. It's not uncommon for teens to make rash decisions and then regret them afterward. For example, traumatized teens might talk about driving too fast or driving while drunk, having risky sex, or breaking rules. Although traumatized teens may be overly cautious sometimes, at other times, their brains are telling them they are invincible. If you have experienced trauma, risky activities might give you a break from negative feelings, because they provide a short-term boost of chemicals that help you feel good (*endorphins*). When we look at the teen brain, the ability to process emotions and think through consequences calmly isn't completely developed until we are in our midtwenties. When making decisions, brain imaging shows that teens use a part of the brain focused on emotion (the *limbic system*), whereas adults use the part of the brain focused on reasoning and judgment (the *frontal cortex*). And older teens actually experience more difficulty with impulsivity than younger ones (Giedd 2008).

What does teen brain development mean for you? It certainly doesn't mean that teens are terrible, impulsive people. It does mean that your biology might be working against you at times. When you are feeling upset or fearful, you might want to change your emotional state quickly, which leaves you vulnerable to taking risks, including using alcohol, driving recklessly, or breaking rules. Understanding and recognizing this process can help you to change it over time. It will also help you to be kinder to yourself, if you have done something you regret. You still need to take responsibility for your actions. But remember, your brain is developing the ability to learn from previous experience and recognize bigger patterns. Chapters 1 and 7 provide some information on how you can better cope with these impulses.

On the other hand, because you have experienced trauma, there is a part of you that's probably very cautious, perhaps far more cautious than your peers. At times, you might feel like your friends are challenging authority, staying out late, or doing risky things, but you do not want to participate. Maybe you have a tough time figuring out if you are too cautious or if your friends are too reckless. You might find yourself going back and forth between being really afraid of people and situations and wanting to take risky chances, just to make yourself feel better and experience that rush of endorphins. Remember that the teen brain is different from the adult brain, and the traumatized brain is different from the nontraumatized brain. If you are unsure whether a situation is safe and healthy, try getting the opinion of someone you trust.

✱ Jaya Says ✱ *I'm a pretty anxious person. Sometimes, classmates or friends do things that I don't want to do, and I find myself wondering if it's normal to be this cautious. It's also hard because lots of adults think all teens do reckless and dumb things. It's sometimes hard for me to find a balance between taking risks and being cautious. I'm constantly asking people if "doing such and such is okay." I know I need to be more confident in my decisions and my actions and not always do things based on other people's approval.*

Facing Fears

Facing your fears is probably one of the hardest things you will do. But the good news is that once you decide that a situation is safe and healthy, you don't have to face things all at once. The process of confronting a fear step-by-step is called *systematic desensitization,* and it consists of several components (McLeod 2008).

The first part is to learn ways to relax your body. It is good to learn these techniques when you are calm and not in the middle of a stressful situation. There are many ways to calm your body down, but the simplest technique is learning deep breathing. When you're afraid or anxious, your breathing tends to become shallow and fast, and the breath goes to your chest, not your stomach. Conversely, relaxed breathing goes all the way into your abdomen, or belly. If you notice the way dogs or babies breathe, you will quickly see that their breathing is often relaxed and deep, going all the way to the abdomen.

The second part of systematic desensitization involves breaking down what you are afraid of. For example, nineteen-year-old David has been afraid to leave his neighborhood alone ever since he was mugged. The first step in his systematic desensitization requires determining if the area in which he wants to walk alone is relatively safe or not (this is where the perspective of a friend or trusted adult will help in determining if his fear is realistic or unhealthy). After adequately learning deep breathing, he develops a *hierarchy*, or a set of smaller steps, that will help him work toward his bigger goal. David gives each step in the hierarchy a rating from 1 to 10, based on how anxiety-provoking each step feels, and he alone will decide when he is ready to move to the next step.

On a scale of 1 to 10, David feels that visiting a new area alone is a 9, which seems pretty overwhelming. So he breaks down his goal into the following smaller steps:

* Walking alone on his own block: 2/10

* Walking alone on his own block after dark: 4/10

* Driving to a different part of town in the daytime: 5/10

* Walking alone in a different part of town with a friend in the daytime: 6/10

* Walking alone in a different part of town by himself: 9/10

The key to systematic desensitization is to slowly face what you are afraid of while simultaneously practicing your relaxation skills (deep breathing). You shouldn't leave the situation until your anxiety has come down to a manageable level—say, a 1 or 2 out of 10. That can take some time. You can also repeat each step as many times as you need to feel calm when you are in it. When you are ready, then you go to the next step. By learning that these situations are indeed safe, your brain is taking in new information and forming new connections, which helps to reduce your fears over time.

Try This! Build Up Your Courage

If you have been avoiding people or places that cause you anxiety, you may want to try facing some of these situations again. Fear and anxiety can become more intense and more broad (involving more people and places) with time. Dealing with fear in small, manageable steps can help you to interrupt this cycle. There are two parts to facing your fears.

1. Learn breathing skills:

    Choose a time and place in which you feel safe. Lie down or sit comfortably in a chair. You can keep your eyes open or closed.

    Rate your anxiety level on a scale of 1 (lowest anxiety) to 10 (highest anxiety).

    Put your hand on your stomach and take a deep breath. See if you can get the air to roll all the way down into your stomach/ diaphragm so that your hand moves up and down as the air rolls all the way into your stomach/diaphragm.

    Take thirty deep breaths.

Rate your anxiety level again, on a scale of 1 to 10.

Practice this one or two times a day for at least two weeks.

2. Develop your hierarchy:

Create a goal. List a situation in which fear is keeping you from doing something you want to do.

Ask a trusted friend or adult if the situation is safe.

Rate your goal on the anxiety scale, from 1 to 10.

Think of smaller steps to help you work toward your goal. Ask a trusted friend or adult for help if you are having trouble coming up with smaller steps.

Rate each of these steps on the anxiety scale, from 1 to 10.

Start with the easiest step and use your breathing when you are in the situation. Make sure you do not leave the situation until your anxiety is down to a 1 or 2. This may take time.

Repeat the situation many times, until you feel very little anxiety, even when you first walk into the situation.

Proceed to the next step in your hierarchy and repeat the steps above.

This process may take several months.

The process of systematic desensitization takes time and commitment, but you can do it. For many teens, having a professional or trusted adult help them with this process can be very useful. Slow and steady progress is actually the best way for your brain and body to learn new coping skills.

* Jaya Says * *I have certain fears that probably seem dumb or unimportant to other people. One of my fears is needles—getting shots. To me, my fear is real, and I have to go through certain steps to calm myself down whenever I go to the doctor's office. Just the thought of getting a shot makes me uncomfortable sometimes, but once it's over, the outcome is never as bad as I anticipated it would be. I always wonder what caused me to have this fear, but the truth is, I don't know. All I can really do is calm myself down when I feel the panic coming on.*

Bravery Is a Skill

As you learn to face your fears, remember that you are doing an extremely brave thing. Our culture sends us mixed messages about fear. Our favorite action movies are often filled with heroes who are naturally courageous, who don't seem to experience the fear that most normal people do. It's rare for us to talk about how some fear is good, because it keeps you safe. It's equally rare for us to learn that facing your fears is a skill.

Bravery isn't something you are just born with; it can be learned, and it takes time to become good at it. So when you are dealing with your fears, be patient with yourself. On the one hand, it is normal for teenagers to want to take chances, experiment a little, and be independent. On the other hand, it's hard to know what situations are safe and healthy—particularly if you've lived through trauma. Bravery doesn't mean you suddenly find the courage to deal with everything alone, in one dramatic step. It actually involves asking others for help and making slow and steady changes in your life.

✱ Jaya Says ✱ *As little kids, I think most people would watch superhero movies on TV and think,* Wow, I want to be just like them! *We would watch them fly over buildings, lift cars, and stop trains. I've realized now that being brave and strong for real people isn't as simple as it is for Batman. For me, being brave is trying out a new club at school or starting a conversation with someone I don't know very well. As much as I'd like to be able to use powers to fly into a burning building, I know that being brave means something different to me.*

Putting It All Together

Fear and anxiety are complex emotions. Some amount is healthy, but if left unchecked, these feelings can take over your life. Learning to face your fears might be one of the biggest challenges you will ever experience. Luckily, teenage brain development is actually on your side. You are in a good position to incorporate new information and learn new skills.

Additionally, facing your fears isn't something that you have to do all at once. In fact, it's more lasting when you learn bravery over time. With help from others and with a sense of patience and kindness for yourself, you can slowly learn to overcome your fears and safely participate in things you enjoy.

Now that we have talked about avoiding situations, the next chapter will focus on how to deal with emotions you might be avoiding, because that is also a part of healing from trauma.

Our Final Thoughts

Figuring out if a situation is safe and then learning how to face your fears about the situation can be some of the most important work you will ever do. If you can learn to face fears, you can enjoy the good times in your life and also bravely deal with any challenges that life presents in the future.

chapter 6

How Do I Deal with My Feelings?

Trauma not only takes a toll on the things you do, it can feel overwhelming. In addition to avoiding people and places, trauma survivors may find themselves trying to avoid their own distressing feelings. Our thoughts about a trauma may cause strong emotional reactions. Note that thoughts are usually statements (such as, "I am never going to be normal again"), whereas feelings are usually single words ("sadness," "shame," "hopelessness") that describe our emotional state. Many teens try to avoid trauma-related negative thoughts because they are afraid of the feelings that might follow (Hayes and Strosahl 2004). If you are having painful thoughts and feelings and are trying to avoid them, you should know that you are not alone. This chapter will focus on how to identify and express feelings, even difficult ones.

A big reason that teens try to avoid negative feelings, particularly anxiety or sadness, is the fear that these states will overwhelm them. Perhaps you are afraid that you will break down or you worry that you won't be able to do anything—like go to school or talk to others. These fears are understandable. No one wants to feel bad if they can help it. The problem with pushing away negative feelings is that this strategy doesn't work in the long term. Either they come back even stronger, or we spend so much time running away from our feelings that we are unable to enjoy life (Hayes and Strosahl 2004). Pushing away your feelings can result in:

* Constant worry or anxiety

* Difficulty enjoying happy situations and feeling positive emotions

* Difficulty feeling any emotion at all

* More intense and painful reactions at a later time

* Difficulty concentrating

* Alcohol or drug use to numb your emotions

* Overuse of technology (video games, social media) to numb your emotions

How We Learn About Our Feelings

Our ability to deal with negative feelings is often a lot stronger than we think, but it takes practice. When you are constantly running away from strong feelings, they have power over you. For example, perhaps someone has hurt you physically—maybe a parent or someone you have dated. In the beginning, you probably had a reaction of shock, anger, betrayal, fear, sadness, or a mix of these emotions. The terrible thing about trauma is that the perpetrator may tell you that you are overreacting or that your feelings are not valid. They may constantly tell you that you provoked their anger, that you deserved the abuse, or that you are unworthy or unlovable. This makes you doubt your own judgment. In time, you learn to disregard your own feelings, thinking they are not valid anyway. In addition, when you have painful feelings, you might learn that they just lead to more suffering, so you try to find ways to avoid your feelings. Eventually, you might find that you have difficulty experiencing any feelings at all, also called *emotional numbness* (Wagner and Linehan 2006)

Allowing yourself to feel is a leap of faith. Maybe you have learned not to trust your feelings. Maybe you believe that your feelings will be too much to handle. Maybe you do not feel worthy of experiencing positive things. None of that is true. If you feel emotionally numb, you can start to reconnect with your feelings in small steps. When you learn to swim, you don't jump off the diving board on the first day. A good swimming teacher will start you off in shallow water and gradually coach you through more challenging tasks (like treading water or putting your face under the water). Learning to experience and express feelings can be thought of in a similar way.

Emotions and Feelings

Most teens don't have trouble identifying *emotions*, which are actually more basic than *feelings*. Emotions are often "hardwired" into the brain's and the body's response to events. If a tiger chases us, for instance, we feel afraid. If someone passes away, we feel sadness. Some basic human emotions are:

* Anger

* Disgust

* Fear

* Happiness

* Sadness

* Surprise

Within each one of these basic emotions, there are many words the brain uses to describe our basic emotions in more detail—these words are our feelings. Feelings give added meaning to what your body is experiencing. For example, depending on the circumstances of someone passing away, you may describe your sadness as "sorrow." And when you're experiencing the basic emotion of fear, you may describe your basic emotion with the word "shock." Learning to identify your feelings can help you make better decisions, to ask for help when you need it, and to stop avoiding things because you are afraid of negative emotions (Linehan 1993). Basically, you can think of strong emotions like waves. You can fight the waves, or you can learn how to surf on them. The next activity will focus on skills to do that.

Try This! Experience Your Feelings

Learning to tolerate feelings, even difficult ones, is a key part of healing from trauma. Feelings don't last forever. Instead, they are like waves that come and go on the water. Some are strong and some are weak, and none of them last forever.

To practice getting in touch with your feelings, choose a safe place. Keep a pen and paper handy as you imagine yourself on a surfboard, riding the waves of your feelings.

- Set a timer for three minutes.

- Allow your thoughts and feelings to wander.

- Imagine that the thoughts are like waves. Some thoughts may have strong feelings that come along with them. That is okay. Remind yourself that you do not need to get involved in each thought. You are on a surfboard.

- As the thoughts come at you like waves, your job is to just label each wave with its accompanying feeling as you continue to surf. For example, the thought *I feel so horrible that this happened to me* might be labeled with a wave called "anger." *I wonder if I can ever get over this?* might be labeled "sadness." *These three minutes sure are long!* might be labeled with "boredom." And *I have to study for my test,* might be labeled as "worry."

- Surf the waves for three whole minutes.

- When the timer goes off, take several deep breaths.

At the end of this exercise, you can write down your thoughts. Was this easy or difficult for you? Did you feel safe or unsafe? What would help you do this again in the future? Also, if you are someone who prefers expressing yourself in a different way, try drawing a picture of the waves you experienced. In the end, you want to allow yourself to experience feelings but to understand that the feelings will pass with time.

✳ Jaya Says ✳ *Feelings are things that I find hard to understand sometimes. When I'm feeling sad or angry about something, one thing that will make my emotions much worse is if someone around me says I'm just overreacting. I see this happen to other people sometimes, and I try not to judge them, because I don't know why they're so upset. So I'm not going to tell them to "get over it" and make their emotions invalid. Emotions can be hard to understand and navigate sometimes.*

How We Learn About Emotion

As we discussed, we learn not to express our feelings when others, particularly perpetrators, tell us our reactions are not valid. Our families and the world around us also give us messages about how to express emotion (Morris et al. 2007). Some families are expressive. Parents in these families express pride in their kids, talk openly when there is conflict, and communicate about disappointment, hurt, and sadness. In other families, emotions are not discussed openly. Kids from these families learn that verbal disagreement is worse than keeping your emotions to yourself—a tendency called *emotional avoidance*. If family members do not learn how to discuss feelings of hurt, disappointment, fear, or sadness, resentments can build up over time and family members may not feel close to one another.

If you come from a family that does not express feelings, it's probably extremely challenging to allow yourself to feel and express emotion. It is also very important work. Emotional skills are the key to having close relationships with others and being able to deal with the challenges of life.

In addition, our larger culture sends us messages about emotions. When we think of "emotionally strong" individuals, we might think of people who keep their problems to themselves or people who don't get upset. Although things are changing, we do not come from a culture that is comfortable with negative emotions. When someone is crying in public, people's first instinct is to look away rather than to go toward that person and offer assistance and comfort.

In addition, there are gender expectations about what kinds of feelings are acceptable. Some people think that boys shouldn't express emotions like sadness and hurt, and that girls shouldn't show anger. Of course, none of this makes any sense. We know that males and females both experience all these emotions.

Don't be afraid to be who you are and to take care of yourself emotionally. Eventually, you may become a trailblazer and role model for others as our culture becomes even more aware of the importance of emotional health.

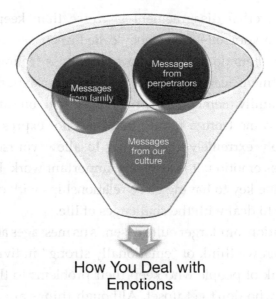

Messages from family

Messages from perpetrators

Messages from our culture

How You Deal with Emotions

Janice: *"I don't want to look needy."* *Eighteen-year-old Janice moved out of her parents' house after high school and started working as a receptionist. Her father was an alcoholic, and her parents often fought with each other, both verbally and physically. When Janice was younger, she would try to defend her mother from her father, but her father would hit her if she got in the way. Over time, Janice learned that if she stayed upstairs in her room, her parents would leave her alone. She would pretend that she was by herself, someplace completely safe. At school or with friends, Janice learned not to express her emotions or talk about what she was dealing with at home.*

After Janice moved out, she started to feel very lonely. Now that she was out of school and on her own, she began to realize that she had no close friends. After a few months,

Janice realized that she needed help. Because her job did not offer health insurance, Janice could not afford to get therapy. Instead, she decided to call a local hotline for survivors of domestic violence and ask if they had services for children who had witnessed violence. With the encouragement of a counselor, Janice became more involved in volunteering in her community and started to make friends. Eventually, she told a few of her new friends what she went through as a kid, and she found them to be supportive. Janice still finds it difficult to allow herself to feel and express emotions, but she knows it is important to keep trying.

✳ **Jaya Says** ✳ *At school and in public, most people I know almost wear a "mask" to hide their emotions and what they are feeling. At school, I know I put on a mask myself because when a teacher asks how I am, it's not really acceptable to respond with "sad" or "angry" or "annoyed." People always expect us to respond with "fine," even if we really aren't. I find it a little confusing as to why you would ask someone how they are if you only expect one answer. I suppose that responding with any answer other than "fine" would make the other person uncomfortable. I wish we had more freedom to answer truthfully.*

Try This! Put a Word on Your Feelings

Over the next week, carry a notebook with you, or simply take notes on your phone or other electronic device. Pick a time every day when you will "check in" with your emotions. You can set a reminder for 4:00 p.m. every day, for example. At that time, just write down two or three words to describe what you're feeling. Some things to keep in mind:

- Feelings are usually one word ("bored," "happy," "frustrated," "irritated").

- You might be feeling a few things at the same time.

- There is no right or wrong way to feel.

As you look back on the emotions you listed, were there emotions that you had difficulty identifying? For example, maybe you have trouble figuring out when you are irritated? Or perhaps you identify anger more easily than fear? The goal of this exercise isn't to change your emotional state. It is just to learn to identify your feelings so that you'll be better able to express them to yourself and to others.

If you want to learn even more about your emotions, try repeating this exercise for another week, but at a different time of day this time. Perhaps you will notice that your mood varies depending on the day of the week and time of day.

Using Imagery to Deal with Difficult Emotions

Emotions have great power over us, partially because most of us have difficulty finding ways to put some "distance" between ourselves and what we are feeling (Hayes and Strosahl 2004). Think about how we talk about emotions. Let's look at the statement "I am sad." If we turned that sentence around ("Sadness is me"), does it feel as true? Maybe not. Sadness is part of what we may be feeling at a given moment, but it is certainly not the whole of who we are. Maybe we are a son or daughter, a student, a basketball or violin player, someone who loves pizza, a person who gets irritated. Clearly, sadness is only one aspect of things. Imagery and metaphors can help us to gain some distance between ourselves and our emotions. That doesn't mean that we are trying to avoid what we are feeling. It only means that we can understand that emotions don't last forever and that they do not define who we are.

So how can you come up with a great metaphor to help you with your emotions? Think about the last time you read a good book or saw a great movie. One of the reasons you remember it is probably because it had great images and a take-home message that could be summarized easily. When we deal with emotions, coming up with something similar—a short take-home message associated with a great image—can be very useful. When you are feeling lots of strong emotion, whether it is positive or negative, a good metaphor can give you the strength to realize that emotions will not overwhelm you and that you can survive your own feelings. The key is to come up with a metaphor that works for you.

Try This! Create a Metaphor for Feelings

A good metaphor is easy to visualize and will illustrate that although feelings can be strong and persistent, they don't last forever. A good metaphor will also illustrate that painful or negative feelings do not need to define who you are—they are only one aspect of what you are feeling, at a certain time. Choose a metaphor from the list below or come up with your own metaphor to represent this idea that your emotions don't have to define you.

- Imagine you are sitting at the edge of a riverbank. Your thoughts and feelings are like leaves and bits of wood that flow down the river. You are on the bank, watching them go by at various speeds, depending on the current.

- Imagine you are swimming and a strong current suddenly comes in. Instead of fighting against the current, you remain calm and tread water. Eventually, the current—like a difficult emotion—passes, and you are still swimming.

- Imagine you are in the middle of a tunnel. Although you might feel like you want to stop your car and exit, you realize you have to keep focused and drive until you see the exit. Although it can be very challenging to stay with difficult and scary emotions, by learning to go through them, you are able to drive toward your goals.

Maybe one of these metaphors will work for you. Or perhaps you can think of another metaphor that allows you to see that strong, negative emotions come and go—that you don't have to be defined by your emotions. Once you find something you like, write it down or put it in your phone. Perhaps you can use it as a screen saver or as a daily reminder. A good metaphor can help you to start thinking about difficult or painful emotions in a very different way. If you really like this technique, there are books that can give you more information about this method (see, for example, Bailey, Ciarrochi, and Hayes 2012; and Spradlin 2003).

Putting It All Together

Avoiding emotions is a common way to deal with trauma. Many teens have received messages about how to express emotions.

Perpetrators, family members, and our larger culture and community may discourage us from expressing difficult emotions. Remember that avoiding emotions doesn't work well in the long run. It prevents you from forming close relationships, interferes with your ability to experience positive emotions, can affect your concentration, and prevents you from trusting your own reactions. Allowing yourself to experience all kinds of feelings is a key part of emotional health, and it will get you one step closer to your future goals. The next chapter focuses on the difficult emotion of anger. We will discuss how your future goals can help to transform this emotion into something productive.

Our Final Thoughts

We need an emotional revolution. It would be great to live in a world where people encouraged one another to experience emotions, both positive and negative, because emotions do not last forever. Difficult emotions are a part of life, and positive emotions make life worth living. Each of us can start by encouraging and supporting one another now.

chapter 7

Anger

As you begin to identify and manage difficult emotions, you may find that anger is a particularly difficult emotion to deal with. Often, we think that trauma results in emotions like sadness and fear, but it can also lead to anger. This chapter will focus on things you can do to prevent anger and ways to calm yourself down once anger begins. (The discussion on resilience in chapter 10 will also include suggestions for transforming anger and other difficult emotions into something more positive and meaningful in your life.)

The first step in dealing with anger is to recognize how it affects us (Tafrate and Kassinove 2009). In terms of our own thoughts, or the things we say to ourselves, anger can manifest as:

* Quick, racing thoughts

* An inability to focus

* Feelings of irritability or impatience

* A feeling that you are going to do something you cannot control

Anger also takes a toll on our bodies. The emotional centers of our brain are activated, and certain parts of our nervous system prepare to engage in conflict (Mills 2005). During a period of anger we may experience:

* Racing heart

* Sweating

* Shaking

* Shallow breathing

Finally, short episodes of anger, or being angry most of the time, can affect our behavior. High levels of anger can lead to:

* Verbal arguments with friends and family

* Risky behavior (driving too fast, abusing drugs and alcohol)

* Withdrawing from others

There is a difference between anger and *aggression* (Tafrate and Kassinove 2009). Aggression can involve physically harming others as well as yourself. In cases of aggression, try to find any adult you trust and ask them where you can get help. The resources section of this book also provides you with some information. If you are experiencing mild to moderate symptoms of anger, such as verbal fights, feelings of irritation, or physical symptoms (headaches, stomachaches), this chapter will give you some suggestions on how to better manage these intense feelings.

Coping with Anger Once It Starts

The sooner you can disrupt the anger cycle, the better off you will be. Now that you understand the signs of anger, try to notice your *anger cues,* which are signs that your anger is building up. For example, if you tend to tense your muscles when you are angry, try to take note of your shoulders at various times of the day. Are they relaxed, or are they hunched over and tight? Similarly, if your thoughts start to race before your body starts to react, pay attention when that starts to happen. Anger cues can include things like faster thoughts, difficulty concentrating, and tension in your body. Once you identify your anger cues, think about how you can break the cycle. You can do things that are calming or distracting, or just try to shift gears and do something totally different. Some things you can try:

* Take a walk

* Text a friend

* Take a few deep breaths

* Watch something on television or play a video game

* Take a shower

* Wash dishes

* Think about how a friend might view the situation and what they would tell you to do

These activities can temporarily distract you from your anger. They give you time to figure out what to do next, including looking at what is behind your anger.

> **✳ Jaya Says ✳** *When someone makes me angry, I have a list of go-to hobbies or activities to calm myself down. I often listen to music; it helps me to relax and tune out the rest of the world for a few minutes, just until I get myself together again. Sometimes, I write stories. I channel my feelings into creating a character or a situation that might be somewhat like mine. I also enjoy drawing or doodling on a sheet of paper, which can be a distraction from whatever is making me angry. Then, I'm calm enough to face the situation again.*

What's Behind Your Anger?

The consequences of chronic anger can be very serious. Unchecked, acting on your anger can leave you feeling lonely and isolated. Perhaps you have been in trouble at home, work, or school. It can be difficult for teens to understand the source of their anger. For example, you might think that an annoying teacher or an unsympathetic parent is causing your anger. This might be the case. But if you experience anger often, there are probably other emotions behind your anger (Parrott 2001). For example, if you've been traumatized, you might become angry rather than admit that you are fearful of a situation. If someone isn't treating you fairly, you might react with anger instead of realizing that you feel disrespected and hurt. If you have a sudden change in your routine, your first reaction might be anger, rather than admitting that you feel sad that you will no longer be able to interact with your old friends.

Alan: *"I am mad at everyone." Alan, a fourteen-year-old boy in eighth grade, lost his home in a tornado. His family had to move to an apartment, and Alan had to change schools in the middle of the year, where he had trouble making friends and fitting in. Although his parents had always had their share of problems, losing their home put a great deal of stress on both of them. Alan felt like there was a lot of yelling and fighting in his house since the move.*

Even though Alan had always been an above-average student, he became very withdrawn. He stopped doing his homework, and he began to start fights. When someone "looked at him the wrong way," Alan would begin to verbally abuse them. After several incidents, the school called Alan's parents. The school social worker began to work with Alan to understand the roots of his anger and to find better ways to manage it. Alan admitted that he felt depressed about the loss of his house and his family, and the fact that it happened "all at once made it really bad."

At his social worker's suggestion, Alan joined a few clubs, and his mother agreed to take him to his old neighborhood once a week to see some of his old friends. The social worker also suggested that Alan's parents work with a professional so that the family could communicate in a healthier, more supportive way. Although the social worker was not able to change the reality of what Alan had to deal with, she helped him explore the emotions behind his anger and to find other ways to cope.

Preventing Anger from Building Up

Alan's story illustrates that identifying the emotions behind anger can help us cope with anger after it has begun. Making calming and enjoyable activities a regular part of your life can help anger from building up in the first place. Consider doing some of these things regularly:

* Yoga

* Counting to fifty while taking deep breaths

* Prayer or meditation

* Writing, journaling, or painting

Try This! Track Your Moods

One way to reduce your overall anger level is to engage in some sort of healthy coping method every day. If you do it regularly, even a few minutes a day can make a difference in the way your mind and body feel.

- For one week, set an alarm for three times a day (maybe at breakfast, lunch, and dinner) at a convenient time.

- Use a notebook or electronic device to write down the emotions you are feeling at those times. Pay special attention to when you are feeling angry and try to figure out if any other emotions (feeling sad, disrespected, hurt, fearful, or lonely) accompany your anger. The goal of this week isn't to change your mood, it is just to observe your patterns.

- For the second week, choose one or more of the healthy activities listed in this chapter. Do at least one of them every day (exercise, breathing, sports, journaling).

- You do not have to do the same activity every day. The important thing is to try to do at least one calming thing every day.

- Just like you did the week before, set an alarm for three times a day at times you choose. Again, write down the emotions you are feeling at those times. See if you notice a change in your anger level.

Remember that it takes several months (about 8–12 weeks) to build up healthy habits, so try to keep doing your healthy activity for several months. Feel free to try different types of healthy activities and see which ones help your mood. This is a personal journey, so you will have to find the best path for you.

Does Anger Define Me?

Maybe other people see you as an angry person. Maybe you see yourself as an angry person. Sometimes, it helps to take a step back to figure out who you really want to be. In your heart, you may not like the way you behave when you are very angry. Taking time to reflect on our own values is important. For example, ideally, how would you like to treat your parents? Siblings? Friends? Boyfriend or girlfriend? Ideally, how would you like to interact with people at work or at school? Also, consider how your community and your religion or spirituality might shape what is important to you. Finally, in a perfect world, how would you want to treat your body? The point is to think broadly about the kind of person you want to be and what is important to you personally. Every person is unique, so there are no right or wrong answers. Behaving in angry ways may be violating your *own* values, not just upsetting other people. If that is the case, the next step is to find other ways to deal with anger.

Try This! Explore Your Values

A powerful way to change your behavior can be to figure out what you truly value. For example, we may value our relationships with certain people, or we may value certain attributes like kindness, justice, leadership, courage, or perseverance. Maybe we value practicing our faith or taking care of people who are less fortunate. Perhaps we value becoming educated or financially successful.

- List three big things you value (for example, a close relation-ship with your mom, being smart, being nice to people). Find a way to remind yourself of these values every day (like posting your list to your bedroom wall or setting an electronic reminder message).

- Now get specific. For each of these values, write down exactly what you're hoping for (for example, not to fight with your mom, to make the honor roll, to help homeless people).

- Consider how you can get there. This is the time to think about what you can *do* to achieve what you want (such as telling your mom that you'll talk to her in a few minutes after your anger level has reduced, studying an extra half hour on the weekends, joining the service club at school).

Part of being a teenager is figuring out what your values are. Trying to find ways to make those values a reality in your day-to-day actions is more challenging. The first step is to be honest with yourself about what you want your life and your relationships to look like. The next step is to figure out a way to work toward those goals. Try to find one or two small and specific ways every day to work toward what you truly value. For example, if you want to practice being a caring person, send a quick message to a friend who is going through a tough time. If you want to focus on academics, take an extra ten minutes to review your homework on weeknights. Making small changes over time is the only way we can honor what is truly important to us in the long term.

Anger Prevention

Healthy Coping Once Anger Starts

Transforming Anger Based on Your Core Values

Putting It All Together

Anger is a natural emotion. When you have been traumatized, it is particularly natural to have periods of anger, but often, there are other emotions behind anger. Understanding those emotions can help you to manage anger. In addition, putting healthy activities into your daily routine and exploring your own values can help you prevent angry episodes. And since you are human, there will still be times when anger might get the best of you. Try to recognize the signs of anger building up in your mind and body, then experiment with ways to calm yourself once anger starts brewing.

Our Final Thoughts

We have all said and done things we regret. As mother and daughter, we have both had our share of anger toward each other. But the most important thing is that we try to learn from each experience and, hopefully, talk to each other, cope differently, and improve—although we will certainly never be perfect!

chapter 8

Depression and Social Support

When you have been traumatized, it is very common to experience feelings of sadness, hopelessness, and isolation. If these feelings last for weeks and months, you might have trouble going to school or work or participating in activities you enjoy. You might also find that your relationships suffer. This chapter will focus on learning strategies to combat depression, as well as on exploring how to nurture healthy relationships and let go of relationships that are not good for you.

Signs of Depression

Every teen experiences periods of sadness. That is normal. However, if these negative moods last for more than a few days or if they are getting in the way of your ability to enjoy your life, then the problem may be more serious. Some symptoms of depression include:

* Increased sleep or difficulty sleeping

* Losing interest in things you used to enjoy

* Feeling guilty or hopeless

* A lack of energy

* Difficulty concentrating

* Overeating or difficulty eating

* Feeling like your thoughts and body are moving slower than you want them to

* Feeling like you might harm yourself

Breaking the Cycle

If you are experiencing these symptoms, there is a lot that you can do to help break the cycle of depression. Decades of research have shown us that our feelings, thoughts, and behaviors are all closely connected, and breaking into this cycle is key in dealing with depression.

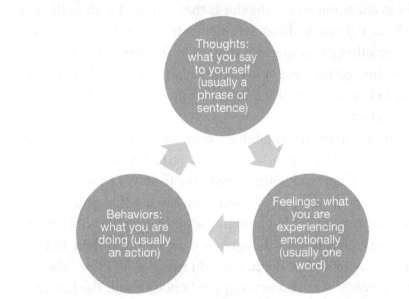

You might be wondering, *How can I change my feelings?* After all, if you could just snap your fingers and feel better, you would. Changing your feelings is not that easy. However, changing your behaviors and thoughts can help you to make changes in your feelings. For example, if you feel hopeless, you might have accompanying thoughts like, *Nothing is ever going to get better.* As a result, your behaviors might then be staying at home and not attending an activity that you used to enjoy.

Changing your behavior can help to disrupt this cycle. You may decide to get up and do your activity, even if you don't feel like it. Once you get there, you might think, *At least I got to see a few of my friends. This wasn't so bad.* Your mood might change from "hopeless" to "comforted," which is an improvement. The key to changing your behavior is that you can't wait until your feelings tell you to do something. Instead, you have to actively do something you might not want to do. For example, sometimes just getting out of bed and changing your clothes helps you feel better, even if feelings of depression are telling you to stay in bed.

In addition to changing your behavior, another way to disrupt the cycle of depression is to try to change your thoughts. Chapter 5 encouraged you to look at your feelings like a lawyer or a reporter would. You can use this skill to transform depression-related thoughts into more balanced thoughts. You can examine your thoughts and figure out if there is a different way to look at them. Are you using words like "always" and "never"? Are you making predictions about the future or saying things to yourself about your character without proper evidence? Consider these unhealthy thoughts and their more balanced counterparts:

* *I am never going to get over this.* → *I feel down today, but no feeling lasts forever.*

* *The future is hopeless.* → *No one can predict what will happen tomorrow. There is a chance something good could happen.*

* *I am a horrible person.* → *I am not a perfect person, but I have done a lot of nice things in my life.*

* *I don't deserve to be happy.* → *Everyone deserves happiness and respect, myself included.*

* **Jaya Says** * *Maybe it sounds cheesy, but it's really true that your mind-set can change how you think. I know that depression isn't as simple as thinking, I'm going to be happy now! However, changing your thinking can be really helpful. I sometimes wake up feeling like I don't want to do anything, but looking at my thoughts differently does help change my outlook on the day.*

Tina: *"I'm not meant to be happy."* When Tina was eighteen years old, she was a high school senior getting ready to go to junior college. Her mother had passed away from cancer when she was only eight, and she was very close to her father. Tina did not have any siblings, so she and her father spent a great deal of time together when he was not busy traveling for work.

One day, Tina received a phone call saying that a drunk driver had killed her father. Tina was able to stay in their house and start college, but over the next year, she became overwhelmed with sadness and anxiety. She became afraid when her close friends would travel out of town, worried that something terrible would happen to them. She worried that there was something horrible about her that had brought bad luck and death to those she loved—first her mom, then her dad.

When she told her close friends about these thoughts, they tried to help her by telling her she didn't do anything to cause the death of her parents. Instead, they told her she was a kind and generous person, which is why they loved her so much. Her friends also made sure that she was eating regularly and attending her classes. They insisted that the routine was good for her.

There is no right or wrong way to deal with a sudden and traumatic loss. Because Tina had already lost her mother at a young age, she had an extremely difficult time coping with her father's death. Her friends were a great source of support because they helped her to challenge her painful thoughts and they kept her active, helping to weaken the cycle of depression-related feelings, thoughts, and behaviors.

Try This! Break the Depression Cycle

Breaking the cycle of depression requires you to think about things differently or to do something different to change your mood. The goal is to practice healthier thinking and activities on a regular basis. Eventually, you may find that feelings of depression are less intense and that they do not last as long.

- The next time you are feeling down, write down the thoughts that are going through your mind.

- See if you can replace some of your thoughts with alternate, healthier thoughts. You can look at the thoughts like a lawyer or a reporter would, trying to figure out if they are true. Or you can look at them like a close friend would, trying to figure out if they are kind (to yourself and others).

- Keep those healthier thoughts with you, either on a piece of paper or electronically. Read them at least once a day and read them when you feel down or depressed.

- In addition to examining your thoughts, try to do something that your depression is preventing you from doing. For example, attend an event, watch your favorite movie, get up and get dressed, eat a healthy meal, or exercise. Remember that changing your behavior can help change your mood.

Thoughts, behaviors, and feelings are all related. By changing one, we change the others. You can use this to your advantage to improve your mood and fight depression.

Choosing Relationships Wisely

Along with affecting your activities, feelings of depression can also take a toll on your interactions with people around you. When you have lived through a trauma, you might feel that people have let you down or that people you love did not offer you the emotional support you needed. After a traumatic event, it can be hard to figure out which relationships you should invest in and which ones you can let go.

One technique that can help us to judge whether we want to continue a relationship or not is to examine our *priorities* in each relationship closely. Every time we communicate with another person, we are usually balancing three different things: getting our objectives met, preserving the relationship, and preserving our self-respect (Linehan 1993). An example will help illustrate this concept. Perhaps we have the goal of getting a specific task accomplished. Maybe you are asking your friend to bring home a copy of your homework because you are sick. In that case, the priority is *getting your goal or objective met* (getting your assignment). You may be less worried about your friend's feelings than making sure that your needs are met (getting your assignment). In another instance, perhaps you agree to bring home your friend's homework even though it is out of your way, because your priority is to *preserve the relationship* with a good friend. In this case, you might do something you don't want to, but because you think the relationship is important, you decide to do it anyway. Finally, maybe your friend asks you to do something you don't agree with, like asking to copy your homework. In this case, you may decide not to do it, because your priority is to *preserve your own self-respect.*

If you are dealing with symptoms of depression, you may feel that you don't have a lot of energy for your relationships and you might feel overwhelmed trying to decide which relationships are healthy for you. Examining the three priorities (getting your objective met, preserving your relationship, and preserving your own self-respect) can help you to figure out which relationships are worth investing in. If someone has been supportive of you in the past and has gone the extra mile to preserve your relationship, it makes sense that you may want to do the same for them. In addition, if you feel that someone (say, the captain of a team you want to join) can help you get a specific need met (getting on the team), you may decide that your objective (joining the team) is important. In these kinds of relationships, you may not be emotionally close, but you may decide to be friendly because of a common interest. Overall, it makes sense to put time into relationships that are emotionally supportive or ones that may help you meet an objective.

However, when someone has not been supportive of you or has repeatedly asked you to do things that compromise your self-respect, you may decide not to pursue that relationship. If someone is abusing you emotionally or physically, or continually makes you feel bad about yourself, you should take steps to end that relationship. Consult the resources section of this book for more information if you need help. After all, everyone deserves respect, and that includes you.

Try This! Relationship List

Deciding which relationships to focus on can be an important part of dealing with depression. We all need someone to lean on during times of stress. We also need people who can help us stay involved in activities, even if they are not our closest confidants. Finally, we need to avoid people who regularly cause us to compromise our self-respect. These people may urge us to do things we are not proud of, or they may be people who put us down on a regular basis.

- List 1: Write down the names of people who have shown you moral support during difficult times.

- List 2: Write down the names of people who can help you meet your short-term or long-term goals—for example, a teacher who is going to write your college recommendation, a neighborhood friend who walks to school with you, or an acquaintance at school who helps you to prepare for a big audition.

- List 3: Write down the names of people who you feel have mistreated or disrespected you. This includes people who have harmed you physically or emotionally, those who disbelieved you when you told them about your trauma, or those who regularly disparage you in some other way.

- Draw a large X through the names in list 3. You do not need to invest emotional energy in people who do not respect you. In the remaining two lists of names, underline which relationships are most valuable to you. Be sure to underline at least one name in both list 1 and list 2.

- Decide how you can nurture these relationships in the next week. Perhaps you can text to say hello or send a thank-you, or you can ask your friend to have lunch or go shopping with you. The goal is simply to initiate some contact (however small) with a few people who are important to you.

Overall, deciding which relationships to focus on will help you to build up your support network over time. And deciding which relationships are damaging to your self-respect can also be an important way to combat feelings of depression and hopelessness. Although you do not have total control over the people you see in your life, you can decide which relationships are important. You deserve relationships with people who treat you well.

✳ **Jaya Says** ✳ *Sometimes I get close to people, and I wonder if they actually like me or if they just like the things we have in common. Sometimes, they'll say something that is a little hurtful, and I won't know if it's a joke, so I shrug it off until they make more "jokes." These types of friendships are sometimes hard to navigate. It's important to know who is really there for you and who isn't.*

Putting It All Together

Depression is a common reaction to trauma. Because thoughts, behaviors, and feelings are all related, we can disrupt the cycle of depression by working to change some of our thoughts and behaviors. Although this is challenging, it is also an extremely powerful technique. When you feel depressed, your relationships often suffer. Healthy relationships can provide you with moral support or practical support toward your goals. Letting go of relationships that continually undermine your self-respect is another way to improve your mood and decrease feelings of hopelessness.

Our Final Thoughts

Developing new ways of thinking and behaving is challenging, especially when you are feeling down. Remember that you are worthy of love and respect, and when you find people who love and support you, be sure to treasure those relationships.

chapter 9

Anxiety

After a trauma, it is normal to have periods of anxiety. Anxiety is often one of the most difficult symptoms for teens to deal with. Feeling out of control and worried can take a toll on your schoolwork, friendships, and ability to function. Chapter 4 focused on how you can deal with specific forms of anxiety—namely, trauma-related thoughts, flashbacks, and nightmares. Teens who have experienced trauma may also be generally worried about life and their future. This chapter will focus on how to recognize and manage anxiety that influences your daily life. We will review the importance of preventing anxiety and explore ways you can stop anxiety from building up once it starts.

Recognizing Anxiety

Everyone feels nervous or worried from time to time. For example, it is perfectly normal to be worried about an upcoming test or nervous before trying out for a sports team. Most teens worry about dating and making new friends. Worry about something specific (a doctor's appointment, speaking in public) is called a *fear*. *Anxiety*, however, is an overwhelming sense of worry and dread, and it may not always be caused by something specific. It is common for teens who have experienced trauma to experience a high level of overall worry. Teens who have experienced trauma may:

* Feel nervous or on edge a lot of the time

* Feel like something terrible is going to happen, even when they are in a safe environment

* Experience physical symptoms like increased heart rate, rapid breathing, shaking, and sweating

* Have difficulty concentrating

* Have difficulty sleeping

* Experience frequent stomachaches, headaches, or tension in the body

* Avoid people or places that cause them to worry

Anxiety Prevention

One of the best ways we can deal with anxiety is to prevent it from building up in the first place. If we practice ways to calm our body down on a regular basis, then we will be better equipped to manage periods of anxiety when something difficult happens. Here's an example. If you usually maintain a healthy weight but then gain a few pounds unexpectedly, you can always go back to eating well and exercising to bring your weight back down. Similarly, if you regularly practice healthy habits, a stressful situation will feel more manageable when it arises, because you'll already have the skills in place to handle things.

Many lifestyle changes can decrease your baseline level of anxiety, such as:

* Reduce your caffeine intake. That includes caffeinated soft drinks and energy drinks, not just coffee.

* Reduce your alcohol consumption. Although alcohol may calm you down in the short term, it can actually cause you to become more anxious as the alcohol is wearing off.

* Reduce your sugar intake. Too many sweets and sugary beverages can lead to a short-term boost that can leave you feeling anxious, then tired.

* Go to sleep and get up at around the same time every night. It is okay to sleep in on the weekends, but try to get up within an hour of your regular waking time.

* Exercise at least three times a week for half an hour. You can decide if you want to exercise moderately or break a sweat. Exercise can change your brain chemistry and help you deal with both anxiety and depression.

Deep Breathing

One of the most powerful anxiety management tools is deep breathing. Obviously, we all breathe! But the key is to learn how to breathe deeply. As we discussed in chapter 5, learning to breathe all the way into your diaphragm (or belly) is a great way to calm down your body. The best part about this kind of breathing is that no one knows when you are doing it. You can practice it when you are home alone, when you are in class, or when you are in traffic. No one notices your breathing, and it has an incredible effect on your body.

Teens who are very anxious may be afraid to try to relax. You may be afraid to let your guard down or worried that something bad will happen if you stop worrying. Experiment with deep breathing in a safe setting for short amounts of time. You might find that if you try it slowly, you will be able to build your skills over several weeks.

> Tanya: *"I worry about everything." Tanya, a sixteen-year-old junior in high school, was mugged at gunpoint by a stranger while walking home from school. Her dad died when she was young, and Tanya and her mom are very close. After the attack, Tanya began to experience periods of intense anxiety. She would feel her heart racing, palms sweating, and dizziness for several minutes. She dreaded walking home from school, even though her friends no longer let her walk home alone. Over time, her fears began to take over. For example, Tanya didn't want her mother to drive to work alone, terrified that something terrible was going to happen.*

With her mother's encouragement, Tanya began to see a therapist and decided to reduce her caffeine intake and get on a regular sleep schedule. Her therapist encouraged her to begin deep breathing, doing yoga, and listening to her favorite music. After putting a healthy routine in place, they were able to focus more on Tanya's trauma in therapy.

Tanya's story shows us the importance of establishing healthy habits to help manage anxiety. Taking good care of yourself means you will be better able to cope with the stress that comes with talking about trauma or dealing with difficult feelings.

Try This! Practice Breathing

The good news about deep breathing is that you don't need to do it for a long period of time and you can do it anywhere. You don't need any special equipment either! The secret is to take a few deep breaths several times a day when you are not anxious. Then when you are anxious, you can use this skill to help you relax. When you start your practice, you might want to do it in a quiet and safe place, then build up to a noisier environment in subsequent days and weeks. You can keep your eyes open or closed—whatever is more comfortable for you.

- Put your hand on your stomach and breathe. You should feel your hand move up and down. Once you know you're breathing into your belly and not just your lungs, you can continue the exercise with your hand on your stomach or let your hands rest at your sides.

- Inhale on the count of one and exhale on the count of two.

- As you inhale and exhale until the count of ten, imagine your stomach filling up like a balloon and then deflating like a balloon.

- You can also notice that deep breathing may reduce your heart rate.

- Practice deep breathing one or two times a day.

- As you become more comfortable with deep breathing, challenge yourself more. Try to breathe in a waiting room, in class, or while you are walking home or talking to someone.

The more you practice your breathing, the easier it will become. Deep breathing is a wonderful way to calm your body during times of anxiety.

✳ Jaya Says ✳ *I use my breathing to deal with my anxiety a lot of the time. It's really calming to just focus on your breathing and nothing else for a short time. I usually keep my eyes open but focus on an object around me. I know a lot of people think the deep breathing technique doesn't really work, but I would encourage them to try it a few times and see if it helps with their anxiety, as it does for me.*

Mindfulness

When we are anxious, we are often caught up in thinking about the past or worried about what will happen in the future. For example, you might be so worried that your friend hasn't texted you back that you are not paying attention to someone who is talking to you. You may be nervous about tomorrow's test and forget to listen to the teacher as she talks about today's assignment. On a more serious note, maybe you have moments when you think about your trauma and you have a hard time focusing on what is happening around you.

Mindfulness is a way to come back to the present moment, to put you back into what is happening around you right now. A great way to combat anxiety is to introduce regular mindfulness activities into your life. Any time you can slow down and pay attention to what you are doing is an opportunity to practice mindfulness in everyday life. Here are some suggestions:

* Eat an orange. This involves sitting down with the orange and turning off all distractions—no phones, music, screens. As you peel the orange, pay attention to how the skin *feels* in your hands. Is it rough? Is it sticky? Now focus on the *smell* as you begin to peel it. Focus on your *taste* buds. Is your mouth watering even before you taste the orange? As you taste the orange, pay attention to the *texture*. Chew it slowly and see how long the taste lasts in your mouth.

* Take a car ride. You can be a passenger or a driver in this exercise. Again, turn off all distractions—no phones or music. As you sit in the car, pay attention to the feel of the road under your feet. Listen closely to the sounds of the other cars. Can you hear the wheels of your car? Can you hear the noises outdoors? If the weather allows, open the window and

feel the breeze on your face and arms. Notice the air temperature around you.

Just like deep breathing, which can be used anytime, mindfulness is also an incredibly powerful practice. You can use it anytime and during any routine activity. For example, when you walk home, just pay attention to your breathing, your body, the weight of your feet on the sidewalk, and the feel of the air around you. If you are playing with a dog, pay attention to the feel of the fur in your hands, the movements of the animal, and its response to you. When you practice mindfulness on a regular basis, it can help you reduce your overall level of anxiety.

When Anxiety Feels Overwhelming

As much as you try to prevent anxiety, it is a normal emotion. Telling ourselves not to be anxious usually doesn't work. The good news is that the body cannot sustain a high level of anxiety for a long time. Once anxiety has built up, if you can learn ways to tolerate it and allow it to pass, you may find that the anxiety is actually less intense and subsides more quickly.

It can help to get some "space" between you and your anxiety. When you are anxious, your mind is probably full of thoughts like *Am I going crazy? What is going to happen? Will I always feel like this?* Remember that these are just thoughts being generated by your mind. There is also a part of your mind that "notices" what you are thinking without becoming overly involved in the content of each thought. That part of your mind is still a part of you, but it is an "observer" to your various thoughts.

Developing your observer skills can be useful during times of high anxiety.

Try This! Your Mind as a Conveyor Belt

When you are anxious, it can be very hard to try to detach from all of your thoughts. You may find yourself caught up in the content of each worry. When that happens, your body may become tense, your heart rate may increase, and the cycle of anxiety continues. Learning how to be an observer of your thoughts can help you, especially during times of anxiety.

- The next time you are worried about something, go to a quiet place and allow yourself to worry for a few minutes.

- As you start to worry, imagine yourself working in a factory. Each one of your thoughts is in a box, and your job is just to stamp each one of the boxes with a word or two when it is in front of you. The stamp on the box needs to describe what's in it.

- You get to decide how to label your individual stamps. For example, one of your stamps might read SCHOOL-RELATED WORRY and another might be WORRY ABOUT THE FUTURE. Other labels might include, TRAUMA THOUGHT, BOREDOM THOUGHT, or HAPPY THOUGHT.

- As you stamp the boxes, notice that a part of your mind (the observer) is just stamping the thoughts.

- Pay attention to the feeling of not getting involved in each thought.

- After it is stamped, allow each thought to pass by on the conveyor belt.

By practicing this regularly, you may find it easier to manage episodes of anxiety. Some teens feel that this technique helps to make anxiety less intense and that the anxiety doesn't last as long.

* **Jaya Says** * *I have always been someone who worries. In second grade, I would worry about going to school in the morning. My mom suggested that we use a (slightly embarrassing) technique where we would wake up early and have this designated time to worry and/or cry. Although it seems really strange now, it actually worked, and I would feel better afterward.*

Putting It All Together

One of the ways to manage anxiety is to be kind to yourself and your body. That includes cutting back on caffeine, sugar, and alcohol. It also means getting enough sleep and taking good care of yourself. You can face stressful situations when you are already taking care of yourself. Practicing deep breathing and mindfulness can be a powerful way to prevent anxiety, and the good news is that you can do these things anywhere—no special equipment needed. Finally, although it might take practice, work on getting some "distance" from your anxious thoughts. Everyone has times when they are worried and anxious. Allowing yourself those moments can actually be a good way to cope.

Our Final Thoughts

We are so used to avoiding our anxiety that it can be hard to allow ourselves to be anxious. We both worry about things, and sometimes giving each other the support and the space to be anxious actually helps!

chapter 10

Hope, Resilience, and Growth

This book has covered many topics. Together, we've discussed how to live a healthier life, how to deal with blaming yourself, and how to manage symptoms like flashbacks, nightmares, anger, depression, and anxiety. Trying new things can feel scary and overwhelming. But as a teen, you also have the ability to learn and to change. Your brain is changing rapidly, and your ability to absorb new information is at its peak. While the terrible things you have experienced will always be a part of your story, they don't need to define who you are. This chapter will explore how you can survive and thrive after a trauma. You deserve to live a fulfilling and meaningful life. And remember, with the right skills and support, you can do just that.

Resilience

You have survived something incredibly difficult. Trauma changes your view of the world, your relationships, and your sense of who you are. But there is also life after trauma. You can acknowledge what you have survived but still make room for many positive experiences as your life continues. *Resilience* is the ability to adapt after living through one or many traumatic events (Horn, Charney, and Feder 2016). The things that promote resilience can be internal to you, or they can be things in your environment (Fergus and Zimmerman 2005). Resilience isn't a character trait; you aren't born with it. Instead, you can develop the skills that contribute to internal resilience. These include:

* Making and following through on plans to help yourself

* Finding a sense of *self-efficacy* (a feeling that you can take on challenges)

* Developing the ability to manage strong feelings

Many of the exercises in this book focus on how to break things down into small, manageable steps rather than facing a huge challenge all at once. We have also explored how the things you do (your behaviors) and the things you say to yourself (your thoughts) can influence how you feel. Over time, changing your behaviors and thoughts can help you build up a sense of self-efficacy, which is the belief that you can succeed! Each time you tackle small problems and experience a victory, your confidence will grow. This book has also focused on how to tolerate strong feelings. By engaging in healthy coping, finding ways to come back to the moment (mindfulness), and allowing yourself to view your feelings with some distance, you are also building up your resilience skills.

Some things in your environment also contribute to resilience. These factors can help you cope with adversity and trauma, and they include:

* Parental support

* A relationship with an adult you trust (like a teacher or a coach)

* Community support (programs or organizations that help you if needed)

You may not have all of these factors easily available in your community. You may need to develop a relationship with a trusted adult or find community support (see the resources section at the back of this book) to promote your resilience.

Try This! Build Your Resiliency

In chapter 1, you identified your strengths. Now it's time to decide how you can truly nurture those talents and skills. Resilience skills can focus on your body, your mind, your spirit, and your relationships. Choose at least a few activities (or create your own activity) from the categories below:

- For your body: do exercise, participate in team sports, practice yoga, dance, walk

- For your mind: write a poem, paint a picture, play an instrument, sing, solve a puzzle

- For your spirit: pray, meditate, practice deep breathing

- For your relationships: join activities you enjoy, volunteer to help others, engage in activism to change laws and our culture

Make a plan about how you will engage in the activity or activities you have chosen. The plan should include how often and the length of time for each activity. Make sure to set a goal that you can reach so you can build up your sense of self-efficacy!

Post-Traumatic Growth

In chapter 1, we introduced the term "post-traumatic growth," which is closely related to resilience (Meyerson et al. 2011). As survivors heal from trauma, some report that their experiences have changed them—and that some of their growth has been positive. This *does not* mean that they would want to experience the trauma again if they had a choice. It *does not* mean that they never experience any distress about what they lived through. But it *does* mean that they may have learned how to integrate their traumatic life events into their larger life story.

Post-traumatic growth is characterized by the following:

* A greater belief in your own strength to endure and overcome life's difficulties

* A different perspective on your relationships (including valuing relationships that mean a lot to you)

* A greater sense of understanding for those who are suffering

* An appreciation for the positive things in life (even small things)

* A purpose that is focused on something greater than yourself

Both resilience and post-traumatic growth involve some common elements. First, you have to take care of yourself in a healthy way. That means not using drugs, alcohol, and cigarettes. It means eating well, exercising regularly, and finding ways to experience your emotions in a healthy way. Second, resilience and post-traumatic growth involve finding a greater purpose or doing something meaningful with what you have experienced. Growth almost always involves finding support outside of yourself. Although it is good to rely on yourself, you also need to rely on others in your journey of healing. For some people, that means finding groups that focus specifically on trauma, and for others, it means being active in their family, school, and community. The ability to transform trauma into meaningful action is the key to living through something very painful, and both your inner skills and outer support will help you.

> Matt: *"I will make it through this." Matt is a fourteen-year-old freshman who attends a small high school. In junior high, he realized he was gay, but he didn't tell anyone about his sexual orientation. Unfortunately, in high school, other classmates began to suspect that Matt was gay, and they began to bully him verbally. Over the course of several months, Matt began to hate going to school. Sometimes, he would pretend he was sick, and his mother would let him stay home. When he did go to school, he began to avoid certain hallways, and he stopped talking to most people, including his friends.*

When his grades began to suffer, a caring teacher, Ms. Alexander, asked him if everything was okay. Matt told Ms. Alexander about the bullying he was experiencing, and she suggested that Matt talk to the school psychologist. The psychologist worked with Matt and his parents, and he eventually told his parents about his sexual orientation. Although it took several months to understand and accept Matt, his parents worked with the school to make sure the environment would be safer for him in the future.

The psychologist also supported Matt as he founded the first LGBT support group in his school district. Although the bullying did not end completely, Matt found comfort in other kids who joined the club, and he experienced a new closeness with his mother, who was very supportive.

✱ Jaya Says ✱ *Several people I know have had to deal with trauma in their lives. As tough as it has been, it's been impressive to see them deal with some extremely difficult things in a healthy way. For example, one of my friends talked to her mom after going through something really painful. She started going to a therapist and soon began to reconnect with old friends who cared about her. By opening up to people she trusted, she showed resilience and an amazing level of courage. Similarly, another friend of mine experienced a lot of bullying. Instead of allowing this to define her, she started a club at school to help other kids deal with bullying and get support.*

Alicia: *"I won't be treated with disrespect."* *Alicia is a nineteen-year-old freshman in college. In high school, she was an honor roll student, and she received a full scholarship to attend four years at her state university. In her sophomore year of high school, Alicia's father was sentenced to five years in jail for drug possession. Alicia believed that racism and discrimination played a role in her father's long sentence, and she often felt sad and angry that their family was no longer together.*

When Alicia began college, she noticed that many people treated her with contempt when they found out that her father was in jail. These encounters would often leave her in tears or full of anger. Alicia started to do research online and learned that having a parent in jail is considered an adverse childhood experience, or a traumatic event. She also read that learning to channel your feelings into productive, meaningful activities is a way to transform it.

Alicia began to take classes in public health and law to explore ways she could help people like her father. In these classes, she began to meet like-minded friends who provided her with emotional support. She thought about her future career—someday, she was going to help families like hers— and that became a big source of her motivation to keep going.

Joey: *"This won't define me."* *Joey is an eighteen-year-old high school senior who is well liked in school, active in sports, and has many friends. When Joey was eight years old, he was sexually assaulted by a male coach of his soccer team. After the incident, Joey told his mother what happened, and she immediately helped Joey get treatment and support. His mom decided not to press charges against the coach because she was afraid it would be too hard for Joey to go through, at his young age.*

Over the years, Joey coped with his feelings by pushing himself to work hard in school and participate in activities. Although there were days when he would become down or anxious, he would force himself to participate in his favorite clubs, just so that he could stay active.

As Joey approached his high school graduation, he read an article online about the sexual abuse of boys. At that point, Joey realized that he wanted to do something to honor what he had lived through. He began volunteering as a mentor at a local youth shelter, providing a positive role model for young boys. He loves teaching them things, watching them laugh, and seeing them succeed at small, everyday tasks.

All three of these stories illustrate a different aspect of resilience and post-traumatic growth. Matt had the courage to open up to a trusted adult (his teacher) and was able to transform his experience into a way to offer support to other students. Alicia used her internal skills (researching things online) to discover that what she had experienced was traumatic. She chose to have her experiences guide her into a meaningful and deeply personal career path. Finally, Joey was able to use the resources provided to him when he was young (therapy, support) to later volunteer to help others learn to find joy in the moment. There are many ways to find meaning after a trauma, and you can too.

Try This! Create Your Message

You have something to say to the world. Your life experiences, your strengths, and your relationships all come together to create a truly unique individual. Find a way to remind yourself of your best qualities and your hopes for the future.

- Write down three things you like about yourself (for example, you are caring, you are a good friend, you are a fast learner, you work hard).

- Based on what you have lived through, how would you like to see the world change? (Maybe you want a world in which parents don't fight or no one is hurt or no child is hungry.)

- Look at your talents and your goals and think about how you can get there months and even years from now. Feel free to let your mind wander and dream.

- You can write down your talents and your goals and tape the list to your wall. Or, if you prefer, you can write about what you want your life to look like in the future or draw a picture that represents your ideal future. Get as creative as you'd like.

Identifying your strengths and being brave enough to dream about your future are great ways to grow and create the life you want. You can achieve your goals with planning, support, and practice.

Putting It All Together

Resilience skills can help you to survive and thrive after trauma. Resilience includes the things you tell yourself, your ability to plan, and your support system. Overcoming something difficult can actually build your resilience for future challenges in life. Post-traumatic growth involves the positive changes that can follow trauma, including a deeper appreciation for the smaller things in life and a greater sense of purpose. You have the abilities and talents to truly make a difference in this world. Although what you have lived through was incredibly difficult, you survived. Remember to be kind to yourself every day. Do something to build a healthier body, mind, and spirit, and closer relationships. You deserve it. And the world deserves your talents.

Our Final Thoughts

Every person is special and unique. Everyone has something to contribute to the world. We are incredibly grateful that you've allowed us to be a part of your journey toward healing. We hope you have learned some new things and learned that you are never alone. And we cannot wait to see the positive things you will contribute to this world.

Acknowledgments

Thank you to every trauma survivor who trusted me with your struggles and your triumphs. I learned about courage and resilience from each of you. I am forever grateful to my teachers and mentors, including Rebecca Campbell, Cheryl Carmin, Robin Mermelstein, David McKirnan, Joe Stokes, and Erica Sharkansky, whose compassion and knowledge have inspired me. Cynthia Miller, you knew what it meant to believe in a little girl who didn't always believe in herself. Thank you to my mom, sister, husband, and daughters for your endless patience and support. A special thanks to my dad, whose sense of empathy and justice influences me every day.

—Sheela Raja

I want to say thank you to the people who have opened up to me and trusted me with things they are dealing with—it really is an honor. I am thankful to Mr. Weber for encouraging all his kids to write and Mr. Kannan for giving me the chance to do so in his class. Thank you to my dad, who makes every little thing happen. It does not go unnoticed. Thank you to my sister, who can make the worst day seem okay. Thank you to my mom, for the experience of writing this with you and for being an amazing and loving person. I love all of you.

—Jaya Ashrafi

Resources

Bullying

Pacer's National Bullying Prevention Center: http://www.pacer.org/bullying/resources/

The Trevor Project: http://www.thetrevorproject.org/

Community Violence and Crime

The National Center for Victims of Crime: http://www.victimsofcrime.org/

Dating Violence

Love Is Respect: http://www.loveisrespect.org/

Break the Cycle: http://www.breakthecycle.org/

Sexual Assault

National Sexual Violence Resource Center: http://www.nsvrc.org

RAINN (Rape, Abuse & Incest National Network): http://www.rainn.org

General Resources

National Center for PTSD: http://www.ptsd.va.gov/

ACEs (Adverse Childhood Events) Too High: https://acestoo high.com/

National Suicide Prevention Hotline: https://suicidepreven tionlifeline.org

References

American Psychiatric Association. 2013. *Diagnostic and Statistical Manual of Mental Disorders: Fifth Edition (DSM-5)*. Arlington, VA: American Psychiatric Association.

Bailey, A., J. Ciarrochi, and L. Hayes. 2012. *Get Out of Your Mind and Into Your Life for Teens: A Guide to Living an Extraordinary Life*. Oakland, CA: New Harbinger Publications.

Borreli, L. 2015. "Human Attention Span Shortens to 8 Seconds Due to Digital Technology: 3 Ways to Stay Focused." *Medical Daily*. http://www.medicaldaily.com/human-attention-span -shortens-8-seconds-due-digital-technology-3-ways-stay -focused-333474.

Brewin, C. R., B. Andrews, and J. D. Valentine. 2000. "Meta-analysis of Risk Factors for Posttraumatic Stress Disorder in Trauma-Exposed Adults." *Journal of Consulting and Clinical Psychology* 68(5): 748–766.

Briere, J., C. Scott, and F. Weathers. 2005. "Peritraumatic and Persistent Dissociation in the Presumed Etiology of PTSD." *American Journal of Psychiatry* 162(12): 2295–2301.

Burns, D. D. 1999. *The Feeling Good Handbook*, rev. ed. New York: Plume.

Fergus, S., and M. A. Zimmerman. 2005. "Adolescent Resilience: A Framework for Understanding Healthy Development in the Face of Risk." *Annual Review of Public Health* 26: 399–419.

Giedd, J. N. 2008. "The Teen Brain: Insights from Neuroimaging." *Journal of Adolescent Health* 42(40): 335–343.

Hayes, S. C., and K. D. Strosahl. 2004. *A Practical Guide to Acceptance and Commitment Therapy.* New York: Springer Science & Business Media.

Heim, C., and C. B. Nemeroff. 2009. "Neurobiology of Posttraumatic Stress Disorder." *CNS Spectrums* 14(1, suppl. 1): 13–24.

Horn, S. R., D. S. Charney, and A. Feder. 2016. "Understanding Resilience: New Approaches for Preventing and Treating PTSD." *Experimental Neurology* 284: 119–132.

Janoff-Bulman, R. 2010. *Shattered Assumptions.* New York: Simon & Schuster.

Jantz, G. L., and A. McMurray. 2011. *Overcoming Anxiety, Worry, and Fear: Practical Ways to Find Peace.* Grand Rapids, MI: Revell.

Linehan, M. 1993. *Cognitive-Behavioral Treatment of Borderline Personality Disorder.* New York: Guilford Press.

McLeod, S. A. 2008. "Systematic Desensitization." *Simply Psychology.* http://www.simplypsychology.org/Systematic-Desensitisation.html.

Meyerson, D. A., K. E. Grant, J. S. Carter, and R. P. Kilmer. 2011. "Posttraumatic Growth Among Children and Adolescents: A Systematic Review." *Clinical Psychology Review* 31(6): 949–964.

Mills, H. 2005. "The Physiology of Anger." *MentalHelp.net.* https://www.mentalhelp.net/articles/physiology-of-anger/.

Morris, A. S., J. S. Silk, L. Steinberg, S. S. Myers, and L. R. Robinson. 2007. "The Role of the Family Context in the

Development of Emotion Regulation." *Social Development* 16(2): 361–388.

National Institute of Mental Health. 2011. "The Teen Brain: 6 Things to Know." A National Institutes of Health publication. https://www.nimh.nih.gov/health/publications/imaging-listing.shtml#pub1.

Pace, T. W., and C. M. Heim. 2011. "A Short Review on the Psychoneuroimmunology of Posttraumatic Stress Disorder: From Risk Factors to Medical Comorbidities." *Brain, Behavior, and Immunity* 25(1): 6–13.

Parrott, W. G. 2001. *Emotions in Social Psychology: Essential Readings.* Philadelphia: Psychology Press.

Raja, S. 2016. "Affect Regulation for Military Sexual Trauma." In *Treating Military Sexual Trauma,* ed. L. S. Katz, 81–97. New York: Springer Publishing Co.

Spradlin, S. E. 2003. *Don't Let Your Emotions Run Your Life: How Dialectical Behavior Therapy Can Put You in Control.* Oakland, CA: New Harbinger Publications.

Tafrate, R. C., and H. Kassinove. 2009. *Anger Management for Everyone: Seven Proven Ways to Control Anger and Live a Happier Life.* Oakland, CA: Impact Publishers.

Wagner, A. W., and M. M. Linehan. 2006. "Applications of Dialectical Behavior Therapy to Posttraumatic Stress Disorder and Related Problems." *Cognitive-Behavioral Therapies for Trauma* 2: 117–145.

Yehuda, R. 2009. "Status of Glucocorticoid Alterations in Posttraumatic Stress Disorder." *Annals of the New York Academy of Sciences* 1179(1): 56–69.

Sheela Raja, PhD, is a licensed clinical psychologist, author of *Overcoming Trauma and PTSD*, and coauthor of *The Sexual Trauma Workbook for Teen Girls*. Raja is an associate professor at the University of Illinois at Chicago, where she researches the impact of trauma on health. Raja completed her internship and postdoctoral training at the National Center for PTSD in Boston, MA. She is a highly sought-after national and international speaker, a blogger for *Huff Post*, and a frequent contributor to various print and television media outlets.

Sheela's daughter, **Jaya Raja Ashrafi**, is a high school student who is passionate about social justice and treating children and teens with dignity and respect. She is an honors student and was the recipient of a civic action scholarship, where she learned about how tweens and teens can become involved in the fight against poverty, homelessness, substance abuse, and discrimination.

More Instant Help Books for Teens

An Imprint of New Harbinger Publications